HORSE RACING'S
GREATEST RIVALRIES

BY THE STAFF OF BLOOD-HORSE PUBLICATIONS

HORSE RACING'S
GREATEST RIVALRIES

BY THE STAFF OF BLOOD-HORSE PUBLICATIONS

LEXINGTON, KENTUCKY

LIBRARY OF CONGRESS CONTROL NUMBER: 2008928615

ISBN 978-1-58150-193-3

PRINTED IN CHINA
FIRST EDITION: 2008

a division of
Blood-Horse Publications
PUBLISHERS SINCE **1916**

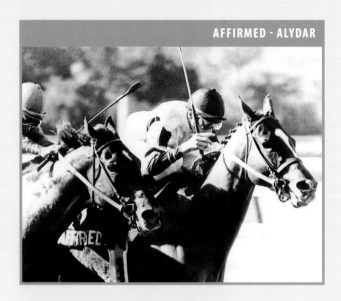

AFFIRMED - ALYDAR

DAMASCUS - DR. FAGER

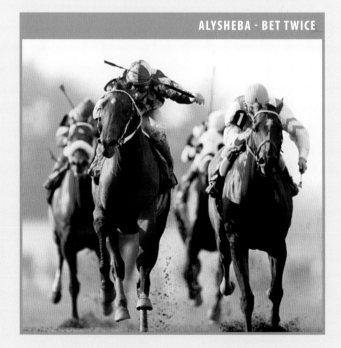

ALYSHEBA - BET TWICE

Contents

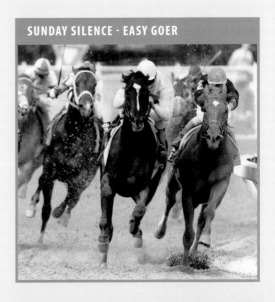

SUNDAY SILENCE - EASY GOER

JAIPUR - RIDAN

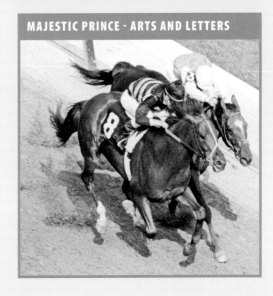

MAJESTIC PRINCE - ARTS AND LETTERS

Introduction

Nothing tests the heart of a racehorse more than a worthy foe whose own courage and relentless challenge bring out the best in both. Colin might have been undefeated, but could he have attained the mantle of greatness without Fair Play in pursuit? Would Dr. Fager have earned the reputation as racing's most brilliant miler without Damascus matching him stride for stride? Or would Personal Ensign's last race have been so unforgettable if Winning Colors had yielded an inch?

Horse Racing's Greatest Rivalries showcases twenty great rivalries, from celebrated match races and memorable Triple Crown campaigns to season-long battles. The rivalries span more than a century, commencing with the famous match race featuring Domino, Henry of Navarre, and Clifford to the 2007 season that culminated in the Breeders' Cup Classic showdown of Curlin, Street Sense, and Hard Spun.

A group of Turf writers and racing historians selected the rivalries as representing racing's best, and the choices validate that contests between and among great racehorses occur in every era and are not just hazy mementos of the past. Some of the rivalries are not as well known as the Seabiscuit-War Admiral match race or the Sunday Silence-Easy Goer battles in the 1989 Triple Crown races, for instance, but are equally compelling. Gallorette and Stymie were the iron horses of their era, with

the filly making 72 starts and the colt, 131. Remarkably, they faced each other nineteen times. Stymie also had separate rivalries with Armed and Assault — bruising battles that earned them championship honors in their own right. The Alfred Vanderbilt fillies, Bed o' Roses and Next Move, contested a nontraditional rivalry in which they alternated championship titles while also racing against males, a practice much more common then than it is today. Nashua, best remembered for his rivalry with Swaps, faced an earlier rival in two-year-old nemesis Summer Tan. And while Silver Charm had the better record, he met his match, as they say, in Free House.

Few things in sports attract more public interest than a good rivalry. Thus, the racing world waits for the next great Affirmed and Alydar to rumble through the stretch with hardly a breath separating them.

CHAPTER 1

DOMINO — CLIFFORD —
HENRY OF NAVARRE

The Domino Effect

BY TOM HALL

The early October sun had at last pushed the morning chill back into the shadows, encouraging a crowd of excited racegoers to forsake the confines of a stuffy New York train station to seek the more inviting accommodations of the boarding platform. Welcoming the warmth brought by a westerly breeze, they waited, anxiously waited, for the 10:10 or the 11:00 or the 11:40 or any other train that would get them to Morris Park, situated in the pastoral countryside of Long Island, in time.

The worthiest of adversaries dueled in a celebrated match race at Morris Park. At the end of nine furlongs, Henry of Navarre defeated Clifford and Domino to claim the honor as the leading Turf star of 1894.

They had come from near and far with the singular purpose of bearing witness to the red-letter event of the 1894 racing year: the date, October 6; the event, a match race starring Domino, Henry of Navarre, and Clifford. The prowess of these three titans of the Turf had grabbed the headlines throughout the year. Inconclusive skirmishes, one against another, during the racing season had piqued the public's fancy. From the union of these two elements — their redoubtable ability pitted against each one's inability to establish dominance over another — sprang a rivalry about to be tempered in the crucible of the fifth race on the Morris Park card.

Domino defined speed. And the speed that defined him almost ruined him before he ever set foot trackside in the afternoon. When Foxhall Keene,

son of noted horseman James R. Keene, saw the almost black yearling colt with the small star and the snip running from the muzzle toward the star, he was smitten. Four thousand dollars later, the son of Himyar—Mannie Gray headed to the hands of Foxhall Keene's trainer, Albert Cooper.

One morning in the fall of 1892, during Domino's yearling training, Cooper tried the youngster in a work at Coney Island. Domino covered the quarter-mile with such blazing speed those clocking the work might wonder if their stopwatches were in perfect order. So astounded was Cooper by this show of speed, he had Domino repeat the work the very next morning. The colt covered the ground just as quickly, but such fast work two days in a row on a still-developing body exacted its toll. Domino

The darling of the public, Domino had been undefeated as a juvenile and had only lost once in sixteen outings prior to the match race.

Because of an injury sustained before Domino began racing, his legs were always of concern and his training required special handling.

bowed tendons in both front legs. Although he recovered, he raced in front bandages ever after.

When father and son merged racing stables in 1893, Domino left Cooper's hands for the training regimen of William Lakeland, who introduced the colt to the racing world. From the outset Domino asserted his brilliance using untenable speed to move from one victory to another with consummate ease. Only on rare occasions did Domino's peers see anything other than his white-socked hind feet. He finished first by a neck once, and by a head once, but he was conceding large chunks of weight in both efforts. In the last start of his juvenile year, Domino dead heated with the powerful and capable Dobbins, whom he had defeated, oftentimes narrowly, on four prior occasions. After

all, though, that was Domino's eighth start and only two days after he had toted 130 pounds to win the Futurity. A little rest and one month later, he packed 128 pounds to a one-length win in the Matron Stakes. Nine starts, nine wins, all at six furlongs, and $170,890 in the Keene coffers. Domino reigned supreme in the East.

But another king lurked farther afield, in the backcountry of the West.

From birth Henry of Navarre had been a colt as regal as his namesake, the brave and bold Huguenot ruler of France. The son of Knight of Ellerslie and Moss Rose was always the favorite at Silver Brook Stud, the New Jersey establishment where he was foaled, not only for his size and beauty but also for his demeanor and bearing. So loved was he that the staff wept to see him led from the farm down the road to Monmouth Park, where he was auctioned away.

These same qualities captured the imagination of a ring full of buyers intent on acquiring this outstanding young prospect, including Byron McClelland, a trainer and owner from Kentucky, who shelled out $3,000 to secure him but had been willing to pay twice that had the bidding demanded.

Henry of Navarre spent the first of his juvenile campaign racing at tracks in Kentucky. His debut at Lexington produced no glowing accolades for his sixth-place finish, but after he won his next outing, Henry took his show on the road, traveling with the rest of the McClelland string to the tracks in the East. At Morris Park he ran up against the buzz saw that was Senator Grady. He lost the next three to that rival although never finishing worse than third. Though he never crossed swords with Domino to gauge his worth, he did meet a juvenile yardstick when he jousted with Domino's formidable rival Dobbins in the Algeria Handicap over six furlongs at Gravesend. The outcome of that race spotlighted Henry of Navarre as more than a mere pretender. He defeated Domino's nemesis by a comfortable two lengths.

Back to Kentucky went Henry with six wins from ten starts and a serious deficit in earnings compared

Henry of Navarre validated his worth with consistent performances during his three-year-old campaign.

to Domino's. However, the following year might prove to be a different story. After all, the distances stretched out and Henry of Navarre had indicated that a brilliant sprinter's speed was not his strong suit but carrying speed over a distance of ground might be more to his liking. Perhaps having not met Domino at his game might prove to be a boon.

Domino had the speed, Henry of Navarre had the looks, and the older Clifford had … well, Clifford had the experience, a year's worth to be exact. As a son of Bramble, Clifford was fairly typical of that line: small, plain, sturdy, robust, and lacking in elegance. Certainly nothing about him would attract the attention of buyers at a sale, so when he went through the auction ring, he brought a mere $900 from W.J. Cherry who, along with trainer Eugene Leigh, had had his eye on the colt. To avoid a bidding duel, the two men flipped a coin to decide who would bid.

When Cherry decided to get out of racing, the yearling passed to the hands of Clifford Porter. The horseman from Lexington, Kentucky, must have held the colt in the highest regard as he named him after himself, hopefully more for ability than for looks. Clifford may have been neither large nor particularly handsome, but he was racy. He ran with an ease and lightness that belied his stout appearance,

his stride professing the incongruous coupling of power and grace.

A trainer on the Western circuit where Clifford plied his trade, Leigh had the opportunity to keep up with the comings and goings of the two-year-old. Clifford received a fair amount of press when he was stolen from Porter's Lexington stable one cold February night and ridden some eighteen miles to

The four-year-old Clifford was a sturdy veteran who rarely finished out of the top three.

Paris before becoming so footsore the thief left the unshod two-year-old in a field. As it was the first theft of a Thoroughbred in Lexington since the Civil War, the event created quite a stir.

After Clifford easily won his first race, Leigh and a partner, Robert L. Rose, bought him for $4,000. That was Clifford's only start at two; at three he won

Billy Lakeland took over Domino's training from Albert Cooper.

lands. Even the official handicapper of The Jockey Club, W.S. Vosburgh, recognized Clifford as one of the best three-year-olds of 1893.

After winning his first two starts at Memphis in 1894, Rose and Leigh headed to New York with the consistent son of Bramble—Duchess. Thus, Clifford, the champion of the West, sallied forth to test his mettle in the East. He would not be found wanting.

Domino, Henry of Navarre, and Clifford — these three bandwagons had rolled down the tracks of the New York circuit in 1894, each success attracting droves of fans that refused to jump off when the occasional loss slipped in. With unbridled devotion to its favorite, each group longed for, clamored for, begged for an ultimate meeting. And the racing association that ran Morris Park obliged. So on this bright October morning the fans gathered, bought their tickets, and waited for a train to take them to see their champion win the day.

Like a high-voltage current, speculation over who would win this ultimate showdown galvanized the passengers, creating a heated debate in one group and reasonable discussion in another. But that's the crux of racing: My horse can beat your horse. Only this time there were three horses of merit.

The Domino camp certainly had its rallying points. Hadn't Domino been a model of consistency? After all, he had won five of six and had beaten both contenders during the year. In fact, he had started the year by defeating Henry of Navarre in the Withers right there at Morris Park when both carried equal weights, and that was after all those rumors about the juvenile champ's lameness and only being a shadow of the horse he was last year. That was our guy's first start, Domino fans asserted, and if we remember correctly, your boy already had four races under his belt and he had won how many of those? Oh, none if we recall.

eighteen of twenty-four starts. He established himself as the most heralded horse on the Western circuit with wins, mostly in sprints, over all the leading horses, such stars as the great mare Yo Tambien.

Clifford's accomplishments scaled the solid fortress of Eastern racing one success at a time. The Eastern establishment could neither deny nor ignore the prowess of this upstart from the hinter-

And, hadn't Domino at scale weights gotten the better of Clifford in that match race at Sheepshead Bay, where he led all the way to defeat the older challenger by three-quarters of a length?

Sure, Domino had thrown in a clunker in the American Derby at Washington Park, a last-place finish against a less-than-stellar field to be sure, but there was a reasonable explanation for that. He had shipped to the West and had arrived a bit worse for

Byron McClelland, an astute Kentucky horseman, owned and trained Henry of Navarre until he sold the colt to August Belmont.

wear. Had he been shipped earlier and had time to acclimate, things would surely have been different. He was off his feed and lacked a bit of conditioning, and Lakeland probably should have scratched him. But, then again, they had shipped him all that way.

And, didn't Domino, after a short vacation, come back as strong as ever, winning four in a row. As for this race coming up, just remember: Domino always delivers!

But, counterpointed the Henry of Navarre fans, the Withers was certainly not a landslide victory. Domino barely edged Henry by a head. And, besides that, not to make excuses, but had Henry been given a better ride by Garrison, the other head might have worn the crown. All the newspapers said so.

True, Henry did have more seasoning going into the race and had no wins for the year, but three of those four starts were against the cream of the older horses and Henry certainly had held his own. He had finished second in three of those efforts and had only been beaten a length by that good handicap horse Dr. Rice in the Brooklyn Handicap. By the way, wasn't that second a feat never before achieved by a three-year-old in this country? Oh, and wasn't Clifford in that race too? And didn't he finish an also ran, so far back he might still be running?

And haven't you conveniently ignored the fact that Henry dead heated with Domino just three weeks ago in the Third Special at Gravesend? So the gap between them, if indeed there is any, except in your estimation, is narrowing.

Another thing, anytime the distance has been longer than a mile, your boy hasn't had everything exactly his way: the 1½ miles of the American Derby, Domino last in a field of nine; the 1⅛ miles of the Third Special, a dead heat and with whom? Lest you forget, today's race is how far? Your boy might just be traveling on the periphery of his pedigree. To be sure, Henry might not have the turn of foot of either Domino or Clifford, but he certainly will have no trouble with the distance.

After all, Henry won the 1⅛ mile Belmont Stakes right there at Morris Park and hadn't he won ten of eleven since the Suburban back in June? Granted, he was fifth in the Suburban, but his fifth-place finish in that race against older horses was certainly better than Domino's last-place finish against his fellow three-year-olds.

And, by the way, did we mention the recent dead heat with Domino, and let's put the emphasis on that word recent?

Unable to stand any more, the Clifford supporters chimed in, voicing support for their stalwart soldier. The Brooklyn Handicap had indeed been disastrous, but Clifford, although favored, had had all chance taken away with a horrible start. As you Domino and Henry of Navarre supporters know, he was left at the post, both literally and figuratively.

He certainly had accounted himself well since then. Sure, Domino had beaten him in the match race at scale weights, but that was only a half-length loss, not exactly a drubbing. But for a move here or a burst of speed there, the outcome might have been different. And that was at a mile. At this longer distance, Clifford might

have the running style that will allow him to carry his speed better and farther than Domino.

True, Domino did beat Clifford on the fair and square, but that was back on September 6, and hadn't Clifford two weeks later defeated Henry of Navarre carrying the same scale weights only a week after Domino and Henry ran the dead heat? This race might just be too close to call, and you certainly can't count Clifford out.

So continued the great debate, throughout the

John W. Rogers guided the fortunes of the consistent handicap horse Clifford after Robert L. Rose became sole owner.

Beautiful Morris Park, the Newmarket of America, hosted the most important event in American racing in 1894: the match race featuring Domino, Clifford, and Henry of Navarre.

length of the journey. As the ardent followers of one camp tried to convince the opposing sides the worth of their argument, the combatants rested comfortably in their stalls, waiting to enter the proving ground.

Less than a cumulative length, that's what separated these three rivals. In June, Domino had taken the nod from Henry of Navarre by a head. In September, Domino had beaten Clifford by three-quarters of a length. Six days later Henry of Navarre had dead heated with Domino. The following week Clifford had edged Henry by an infinitesimal nose. The outcome on October 6 was anyone's guess.

Morris Park rivaled the magnificent tracks of Europe, South America, and Australia. The expansive facility lay on 330 rolling acres edged with woods. The grandstand rested atop a hill and the magnifi-

cent Pompeiian-styled, five-tiered clubhouse stood just to its south. Referred to as the Newmarket of America, Morris Park presented the ideal setting for such an auspicious occasion and had put on its finest autumn dress to welcome its visitors.

And come they did. By train, by trolley, by horse-drawn, coach, even by foot. By any means of conveyance that would get them there. More than 25,000 streamed through the widely flung gates, all anticipating the fifth race on the card. The track was fast; the weather, fine; the anticipation, feverish.

Patiently the multitude waited and wagered through the first race and the second. By the time the horses went to the post for the third race, the Matron Stakes, the crowd's anticipation for the main event had expanded exponentially. When

More than 25,000 racing fans thronged the track to witness Henry of Navarre prevail by three-quarters of a length.

James R. and Foxhall Keene's Agitator, ridden by Fred Taral, came home first, the Domino fans savored the victory as an omen of good fortune and cheered the winner loudly.

In the following race the Clifford connections of Willie Simms, the jockey scheduled to ride Clifford, and trainer J.W. Rogers, who had assumed the conditioning of Clifford when Rose bought out his partner, teamed up in the Manhattan Handicap. When Simms guided Sir Excess to the win, the Clifford faithful took heart.

As the preliminary warm-ups for the fifth race approached, the crowd moved toward the rail to watch the combatants stretch their legs. Henry of Navarre, a McClelland stable lad in the saddle, performed in a most perfunctory manner. It was game day. Henry knew what he had to do, what he was expected to do, and he was all business.

Clifford followed shortly after. He too was piloted by a stable lad and cantered at a fair pace but with such spirit and verve he received a significant round of applause from his many admirers gathered at the rail.

Domino, the darling of the fans, appeared last, and all eyes were fixed on "the Black Whirlwind," perhaps looking for an indication that he was less than perfect. Rumors had always abounded about his legs and the magnificent job Lakeland had done in keeping the colt together. But Domino was stabled here, at Morris Park, not at the Keene compound at Brighton Beach, right between the track on one side and the ocean, where soothing sea air and the therapeutic surf lay right outside the door. Lakeland was known to stand Domino in the salty, cold Atlantic waters every day. However, no sign of anything amiss was evident, and Domino moved through his warm-ups with power and strength, tugging and pulling the lad on his back, who managed to keep a strong hold.

Henry of Navarre came first from the warm-up to the wooded saddling paddock, the beautiful chestnut glistening with sweat and reflecting fleeting glimpses of sunlight as he moved to his spot beneath the trees. He knew this routine well and turned not a hair at the crowd gathered to see him prepare for the race. He stopped for a moment and stood statuelike. A commanding presence, he raised his head, flared his nostrils slightly, and surveyed his subjects with a regal eye, before moving to his waiting grooms.

Clifford followed suit, but the normally stoic, professional veteran of the Turf wars, the blood still coursing through his veins from the warm-up and the applause of the crowd, tossed his head and fidgeted, constantly tap-dancing the ground and nipping at those around him.

Eschewing the chaos of the paddock, Domino returned to his stable to be attended to and not without reason. The saddling of Domino often proved an adventure. In all but one of his races, Domino had been ridden by Taral, a jockey noted for his liberal application of the whip. As a steady result of being the direct object of said instrument's action verb, Domino had developed a severe hatred for his jockey. Upon seeing the anathema approaching,

Domino would react violently, punctuating the air with one or the other or both of his hind heels. Not until a towel had been placed over Domino's eyes would the horse calm down so Taral could mount.

By the time the bugle called Domino, Clifford, and Henry of Navarre to appear, the excitement that had been seething like water heated in a covered pot reached the boiling point and blew the lid off. It was uncontainable. The noise generated by the crowd grew at a fever pitch. In less than two minutes and a nine-furlong journey over the testing Morris Park course, the dust would settle. A champion would be crowned.

Henry of Navarre, carrying October scale weight of 113 pounds, came first to the track, Alonzo "Lonnie" Clayton at the reins. Domino, equally weighted, came second, and Clifford, carrying 122 pounds, was not far behind. The three horses galloped slowly to the post and prepared for the start a short distance apart from each other.

The throng of people around the grandstand could not be contained. A maelstrom of humanity, they moved and swirled to get some kind of position where they could watch the race. Any hapless soul moving some other way was caught in the surge and carried to wherever the wave stopped.

Starts could often be difficult and a good starter was imperative. The accomplished man at the helm, responsible for guiding their fortunes, was James Rowe. The favorite with the crowd, Domino had drawn the inside post with the outsider Henry of Navarre between him and second-choice Clifford on the outside. The three-year-olds were on their best behavior. It was the veteran Clifford who proved sullen and for the first time showed a bit of temper, refusing to start in the first two attempts.

A successful third attempt found Domino and Henry of Navarre breaking together with Clifford in hot pursuit. The quintessence of speed, Domino took the lead with Henry close at hand and Clifford staying in touch with Simms taking a firm hold.

The trio moved through the first three furlongs at a sensible pace for the nine-furlong trip. As they approached the hill, Taral and Domino still headed the vanguard and Clayton had kept Henry in close contact, only a head behind. Both had opened an advantage on Simms and Clifford, who were still well within striking distance.

Once over the hill the running began in earnest. Halfway down the hill Taral asked Domino for his move. Briefly, but only briefly, the black colt responded and for a few strides pulled away from the ever-so-close Henry. As soon as Clayton had seen Domino's attempt at a breakaway, he too asked what was required of Henry of Navarre. Ever so slowly, the chestnut responded and the green-and-gold silks of Byron McClelland inched ahead of the blue polka-dotted silks of the Keenes.

Taral tried the whip but even the stinging, rhythmic tattoos of leather on horsehide could not rouse Domino, and he began to fall behind.

The legion of Domino fans that witnessed the shortening stride of the mighty colt let out a collective gasp of disappointment and tried valiantly to urge their hero forward with their shouts. But all was in vain. Henry of Navarre displayed the turn of foot that had been Domino's hallmark and had beaten his archrival at his own game.

As the pleas of the sorely disappointed Domino crowd diminished with each length he fell behind, the excited exhortations of the Henry of Navarre fans and the pleas of the hopeful Clifford fans began to crescendo as these two horses ran the gauntlet of the stretch.

Almost simultaneously with Domino's faltering, Simms had Clifford in full flight after the disappearing Henry of Navarre, and the Bramble colt was still

Domino, on the rail, led Henry of Navarre in the opening stages of the race while from just off the pace, Clifford kept in close pursuit.

Henry of Navarre earned leading horse honors in 1894 and repeated in 1895.

could only scratch their heads, ponder the reasons for such an uncharacteristic performance, and wait for next time.

Although they would not meet again in 1894, this was not to be the last time the three would face each other. On September 11, 1895, Henry of Navarre opposed Domino in a special race at Sheepshead Bay. A newcomer was added to the mix: Rey el Santa Anita, the upstart who had won the 1894 American Derby in which Domino had finished last and who had just handed Henry of Navarre his only loss of the year. By this time, Henry of Navarre raced in the colors of August Belmont, who had doled out $25,000 to purchase

full of run. Gallantly, Clifford narrowed the gap. His stern determination provided a steely challenge, but Henry of Navarre was made of sterner stuff. In the final furlong Clayton called upon a reservoir of speed and stamina not yet spent, and the bold Henry responded in kind. As the two flashed past the finish post, Henry of Navarre ruled by three-quarters of a length over Clifford. Domino trailed some ten lengths behind, his worse finish since his American Derby debacle in June. The crowd exhaled: A year's worth of adrenalin had been consumed in a heart-pounding 1:52¼.

Hats and canes flew into the air as the winner returned to be unsaddled and the crowd rushed to the judges' stand to welcome the newly crowned king of the Turf.

At day's end the Henry of Navarre fans poured out of the Morris Park gates, ecstatic; the Clifford fans, crestfallen but proud. The Domino fans

him from McClelland. Henry defeated Domino by a neck with Rey el Santa Anita third.

Six days later these three were back along with Clifford and Sir Walter in the First Special at Gravesend. Henry of Navarre again proved his worth with a 1½-length win over Clifford, followed by Sir Walter, Rey el Santa Anita, and Domino.

On September 21, only four days after the last meeting of the big three, Clifford handed Henry of Navarre his last defeat, when he took the Oriental Handicap at Gravesend. Henry finished third, 2½ lengths behind.

However, like a fine champagne that's lost its sparkle, the rivalry of the Turf that belonged to Henry of Navarre, Domino, and Clifford in 1894 would never generate the same excitement and drama as it had for that brief spate of time at Morris Park on as gentle a day as autumn can provide.

Undefeated But Often Tested

Colin scored a two-length victory over Fair Play in the 1908 Withers Stakes, the same rival he defeated by a head in the Belmont Stakes a week later.

BY ELIZA MCGRAW

Sometimes when a certain racehorse dominates a season, the other horses fated to be his rivals are said to exist in his shadow. In the case of Colin and Fair Play, the shadow was more than a figure of speech. For all of Colin's success — and he was an amazing champion, even in that turn-of-the-century time of champions — many victories came with Fair Play chasing him. The brilliance of Colin's light defined Fair Play that much more clearly, so that it is hard to imagine the racing seasons of 1907 and 1908 without the two of them, moving in tandem even as one relentlessly edged the other out.

Owner James Keene, who had also raced the brilliant Sysonby, called Colin his best. It was hard to disagree with that. Colin had his sire Commando's sculpted head and neck and his strong hind end. He also had what horsemen of the day called a "thoroughpin" or "box curb," a swollen area at the inside of his hock that required routine treatment. Never entirely sound, the dark bay Colin made up for any physical weakness with courage and pure speed, and his trainer, James Rowe, and owner made up for it in tenacity. They never backed down from a challenge.

Fair Play also had a formidable owner. He was bred by August Belmont II from two Belmont horses. His sire, Hastings, was the leading sire of 1902 and 1908. Fair Play was a beautiful chestnut colt with a blaze — his bright color reminded people of his maternal grandsire, Bend Or — and matured to 15.3 hands. Like Hastings, Fair Play had a turbulent temperament. This translated to difficulty with handling but also to ferocious competitiveness on the racetrack.

Both racers appeared for their two-year old season in 1907. The unbeaten Colin made headlines all the time with record-setting speeds, but Fair Play was doing respectably as well, with some wins behind him. He had taken the Montauk and the Flash stakes at Saratoga.

On the last day of August 1907, the horses met at New York's Sheepshead Bay racetrack in the Futurity, a race that was both the athletic and social event of the season, held as vacationers returned to the city from their beach and country homes. Fair Play's victories were notable, but his presence in the

Undefeated in all fifteen of his starts, Colin, shown with Walter Miller up, was owned by James R. Keene and trained by James Rowe Sr.

Futurity garnered little more than a footnote with Colin around. It was a brilliant day, with summer's heat evaporating and the promise of autumn's color and temperate weather in the air. Some 40,000 turned out for the race and meandered through Sheepshead Bay's famous grove of trees. They enjoyed the green of the turf, which stood in radiant contrast to the worn, old grandstand.

Colin was a superstar that day, his celebrity appealing to all racing aficionados, regardless of gender. Women, not usually thought of as racing fans at the time, thronged alongside the men in the paddock to see him. Colin's jockey, Walter Miller, had to disperse the adoring crowds to get the horse to the gate.

Colin broke first, with Fair Play right behind him. For a moment, when the horses came to the

Although he could never defeat Colin, Fair Play, ridden by Joe Notter, proved a formidable adversary on more than one occasion.

bend in the Sheepshead Bay course, Chapultepec and Fair Play covered Colin completely, hiding the favorite from sight. "Where is my horse?" trainer Rowe shouted. "Something must have happened to him. They never could have outrun him that way otherwise."

Something had happened: Fair Play. He had made a fair bid and for a moment even eclipsed the champion. Fair Play's backers were to savor that moment, one of the only times in which their colt

grabbed the crowd's attention from the unstoppable Colin. To escape, Colin came around Fair Play, who headed for the rail. On the straightaway, Chapultepec led, with Fair Play and another contender, Meelick, right behind him, almost together. Colin easily came up from fourth place to match Chapultepec, and held off a late bid by Bar None to win by a little more than a length. Fair Play ended up with fourth place. Still, the moment he hadn't been able to see Colin had shaken Rowe, and once the race was over, the trainer thoroughly examined the horse to make sure he hadn't been hurt.

A month later, at Brighton Beach, the two met for the Brighton Produce Stakes, run in muddy going. Colin had no trouble with the conditions and won cantering while Fair Play "ran in the best outside going, as against Royal Tourist, and nosed the latter out in the last stride," said the chart. Fair Play would

Colin won the 1907 Flatbush Stakes by three lengths over the noted runner Celt.

try, running hard with his last round of energy, but it was just never quite enough to catch Colin.

On October 7, the two colts came together for the Matron Stakes at Belmont Park. Colin warmed up in bandages, and racegoers drew worried breaths when those came off; they saw there was an adhesive dressing visible on Colin's hock. The colt's always-suspicious hocks consistently kept fans fretting over his soundness for any given race, and that day, wrote the *New York Times*, "some of the very observing watchers professed to have noticed that Colin did not have free use of the leg."

He was, however, sound enough to head for the starting barrier. They were off. Colin and Fair Play collided and were stuck together for some strides. Colin pulled away then, and even though Fair Play tried to close at the end, Colin won easily yet again, this time by three lengths. Fair Play, the chart said, "came like a cyclone at the end into a decisively fast going second." It sounds as if the "cyclone" should have been a winner, but the even stronger natural force just ahead of Fair Play would not let him tri-

umph. The year 1907 belonged to Colin. He had won every one of his twelve starts.

The colts' first meeting of their three-year-old season drew 85,000 people on a pleasant May 23, 1908, for a three-stakes card at Belmont Park that included the Withers. Colin, onlookers noticed, had not gotten any taller since his two-year-old season but did look fuller and glossy with health. The season was full of promise for the undefeated colt.

Fair Play drew the outside post position, with Colin one away from the inside. Once off, Colin galloped to the front but then briefly lost ground at the turn. Leaving the backstretch, Fair Play and a horse named King James went after Colin. For a brief instant, Fair Play looked like a winner, the kind of horse that could stalk a champion and succeed, especially with Colin's jockey Joe Notter cruising so casually along by the furlong pole. But when Notter heard Fair Play and King James behind him, both under whips, he sat down and urged Colin on. The situation worked to his advantage. Colin still had speed in reserve while Fair Play, two lengths behind him, had already given all he had. Fair Play's slender chance had passed him by. Colin won again.

Colin's steadfast fans were, however, worried about their champion as the time for the Belmont Stakes drew near. The rumors surrounding Colin included that the colt had bowed one or both tendons. Or that he had somehow hurt his leg. But by May 30, newspapers printed stories saying that the horse's injuries were not tendon bows. Now it seemed that the horse must have stepped in a hole, or somehow else wrenched his leg, but no one, including Turf writers, knew exactly what the problem was. Which probably made it that much easier for Colin to be entered in the race at the last minute, even though some said that Rowe had advised

against it. Keene, however, wanted the horse to run, and was not prone to accepting advice. He was famous for his daring and risk taking, making and losing fortunes throughout his career on the track and in the stock market. "It really is difficult to believe a knowledgeable owner and astute trainer would send out a horse with a suspicious tendon on a muddy track, in a heavy rain, 1⅜ miles, 126 pounds against top horses such as Fair Play and King James. But there you are," wrote Kent Hollingsworth in a 1969 retrospective in *The Blood-Horse*.

The Belmont proved to Colin's backers that he was a true racing phenomenon. Here he was, possibly lame or even wounded, and entered in a stakes race anyway. Just to add to the arduous conditions,

Among the top echelon of three-year-olds, August Belmont's Fair Play defeated Hessian and King James in track-record time in the 1908 Coney Island Jockey Club Handicap.

the rain sluiced down that day. The visibility was so bad that onlookers could not even see the field until the horses reached the stretch. At the three-eighths pole, fans could see that Colin was up front easily. Some gasped when they saw how lightheartedly Notter seemed to be riding as he sailed along, worried that he had forgotten that the Belmont finish was farther down than the regular one. He later claimed he was letting the champion conserve his energy and that while he did urge Colin on, the sticky mud and long race had cost his horse some energy by the end. That day, the shadow drew nearest, but a head still kept Fair Play at bay. The race chart confirmed the belief that Notter prematurely thought the race was over. "Fair Play ... stood a long stretch drive in the most resolute fashion imaginable." It almost went without saying, though, that resolute was not enough. Colin won by a head.

Despite the constant heartbreak of Fair Play's relentless losing streak where Colin was concerned, racing fans everywhere seemed to understand that without the beloved undefeated champion, his chestnut rival would have stood a chance. In 1908, the *New York Times* published the placings of horses for the year. "Fair Play Has Ill Fortune Record," read the headline. He ran sixteen times and was never unplaced, but he was "beaten by ill fortune on each occasion," which resulted in a place or a show rather than a win. It was just that in this case, ill fortune had a name and a dark bay face.

Racing itself experienced some ill fortune in 1908. New York had repealed the Percy-Gray Law, which made the penalty for bookmaking nothing more than the forfeiture of the amount wagered. That law had kept horseplayers happy. The repeal, however, essentially made betting on racing illegal.

The sport's popularity declined. But Keene claimed Colin could still fill the stands, even without betting. The park was only about half-full,

Above, Colin had limited success at stud while Fair Play, below, had a stellar career that included siring Man o' War.

though, when Colin won the June 20 Tidal Stakes at Sheepshead Bay.

As it turned out, the Tidal Stakes was Colin's last race. The leg problems — the alleged bowed tendon, the never-perfect hock, or some combination — never really left him. As it did with many other racers, the repeal of the Percy-Gray Law sent Colin to England, but because of his soundness issues, he was never fit to race once there.

With Colin out of the picture, things eased up considerably for Fair Play in the summer and fall of 1908. Of his last nine races of the season, he won six, three in track-record time. Although some racehorse owners sent their horses abroad after the Percy-Gray repeal, plenty stayed home to challenge Fair Play, including King James, Dorante, and Master Robert. Fair Play won the Brooklyn Derby — later called the Dwyer — the Coney Island Jockey Club Stakes, the Lawrence Realization, and the Municipal Handicap. He set a track record at Belmont in the Jerome Handicap, and another one at Gravesend in the First Special on September 19, 1908.

For his four-year-old season, Fair Play's handlers followed so many others in the wake of the Percy-Gray repeal and sent Fair Play to England, where he never even placed in six starts. He eventually went rank, which some blamed on that notorious Hastings temper. Others believed he did not care for Britain's grass racing. In any case, he would not run. In twenty-six lifetime starts, he won ten races overall. His career earnings were $86,950.

After the England disaster, Fair Play came home to Nursery Stud, and three of the five named foals from his first crop won stakes races. He was the first American stallion to sire six winners of more than $100,000 and was North America's leading sire in 1920, 1924, and 1927. He sired 260 foals, 18 percent of which were stakes winners. One of these was the incomparable Man o' War. Fair Play died in 1929.

Colin was no Fair Play in the breeding shed — how can any horse compete with the sire of racing's greatest horse? He was a shy breeder, but he did sire eighty-one foals in twenty-three crops, eleven of which won stakes races. He died in 1932.

The rivalry between Colin and Fair Play would never be a contest of equals, simply because Fair Play never won. Yet his game resilience provided Colin with a worthwhile adversary. During the Belmont, a *New York Times* reporter wrote, "Fair Play, a full length behind Colin at the regular finishing post, was only a half length away when the horses passed the winning line for the Belmont Stakes, though, because of the angle of vision from the grand stand, he seemed much closer." That summed them up: Colin would be forever ahead, but his shadow, Fair Play, always somehow "seemed much closer."

Depression-Era Duelists

BY ELIZA MCGRAW

The thrill of horse racing illuminated the dark early days of the Depression. Many great horses, including Jamestown, Vander Pool, Don Leon, Mate, and Ormesby, were all two-year-olds in 1930. But two colts rose to the heights of this amazing crop and battled each other for the spot at the top. As they struggled against one another, Equipoise and Twenty Grand showed a dejected nation that the most expected defeats sometimes ended in victory and that even the most talented champions have to fight for their glory.

In a rivalry between members of the Whitney family, Twenty Grand, representing the Greentree Stable of Payne Whitney's family, defeated Equipoise, flying the silks of Harry Payne Whitney, in the 1930 Junior Champion Stakes at Aqueduct.

In some ways, the rivals were not all that different. Both were owned by members of one of America's great sporting families. Equipoise was bred by Harry Payne Whitney, who in his lifetime led America's breeders eleven times and topped the owners' list six times. Harry Payne Whitney's sister-in-law, Helen Hay Whitney, bred and raced Twenty Grand under her Greentree Farm name. Both were good-looking colts, and fans nicknamed the refined-looking Equipoise "the Chocolate Soldier," for his rich liver chestnut coat. (The nickname was the title of a contemporary Broadway play.) Twenty Grand was a bright bay, brawny and powerful. Both horses were very well bred. Equipoise was a grandson of Peter Pan, who was also the grandsire of Kentucky Derby winners Black Gold and Brokers Tip, and champion Bimelech. Twenty Grand's sire, the imported stallion St. Germans, had won the Doncaster Cup in England. His dam, Bonus, traced her pedigree back to racing royalty such as Bend Or and Galliard.

These similarities, however, did not prevent fierce competition between the two horses. The races in which they met at two were chapters in a vivid, visceral rivalry, with each fighting to win. Before October 4, 1930, the two were hardly contenders for the same lofty positions. Twenty Grand had respectably won two races, but Equipoise had won six stakes races, including the National Stallion Stakes and the Great American Stakes. The "Chocolate Soldier" seemed poised for enduing triumph.

But that would change at the Junior Champion Stakes at Aqueduct, when the two colts challenged each other. Equipoise was carrying the top weight of 122 pounds, but the crowd was unworried, content to view a day at the races as pure escape from the Depression that troubled their daily lives. They felt sure that their "Ekky" would prevail, and he went off as the 1-5 favorite.

The start went well, and a horse named Rollin In took the lead. Both Equipoise and Twenty Grand trailed the field before the bend, but once they got

there jockey Sonny Workman started whipping Equipoise on. Jockey Charley Kurtsinger had kept Twenty Grand snugged to the rail, saving ground. In the stretch, Workman brought Equipoise to pass Ormesby, who held the lead until the last furlong, when Twenty Grand passed him on the inside and Equipoise passed him on the outside. Equipoise and Twenty Grand were linked briefly, and then in a surge of power, Twenty Grand passed Equipoise in the last sixteenth to win.

Suddenly, the spotlight shifted from Equipoise, and Twenty Grand was news. With the Junior Champion Stakes, "Twenty Grand left no doubt of his superiority," said the *New York Times*. As William H. P. Robertson wrote, Equipoise and Twenty Grand were just warming up for what was to come: "Two of the most thrilling contests in turf annals."

Equipoise relished the mud in the 1930 Pimlico Futurity and edged Twenty Grand.

The first of these was the Kentucky Jockey Club Stakes, run at Churchill Downs on October 16.

The seven starters were away well. Equipoise broke first, with Don Leon second, but Don Leon

Equipoise polished his two-year-old resumé with a handy victory in the 1930 Eastern Shore Handicap at Havre de Grace.

took the lead from Equipoise. Workman brought Equipoise up at the five-furlong pole, and now they were in the lead. Equipoise was "running easily and with clocklike precision," wrote Charley Hatton in *The Blood-Horse*. Twenty Grand was lagging in last during much of the running on the backstretch but then began to gain. As the two horses locked onto each other at the sixteenth pole, the crowd stood and cheered. Now they were yoked together ten lengths in front of the rest of the field, and both jockeys went to the whip. "It was nip and tuck 70 yards out," wrote Hatton, "and with Equipoise at Twenty Grand's withers, it looked for a moment that it might come to tuck and nip. He missed it by about a foot and a half. His distended nostrils were at Twenty Grand's straining throat as they swept under the

imaginary wire." The time was 1:36 for the fastest mile run in America by a two-year-old. The crowd went wild, yelling its excitement over seeing such a display of speed, power, and competitiveness. The rivalry was even more exciting — and heartening — than blind confidence in Equipoise had been. Evidently, racing fans learned, there was no such thing as a sure bet. Anything could happen.

The next "thrilling contest" took place when the rival colts met again three weeks later in the Pimlico Futurity. J. A. Estes wrote a poem about the pair that later appeared in *The Blood-Horse*.

"Then out of the midst of the beaten band/Flashed the purple silks of Twenty Grand/Long-leaping, low in his stride/He collared the leader — I see them yet/The straining muscle and white-whipped sweat."

The Pimlico Futurity was indeed a race worthy of poetry. It was held on a gray and cloudy November 5, the track muddy under dismal skies. Twenty Grand and Equipoise were thrown together with the speedy Mate, who had beaten Equipoise in the Champagne Stakes. Equipoise was running for the first time in the silks of Cornelius Vanderbilt (C.V.) Whitney, who had recently taken over his late father's racing stable. The crowd applauded when it realized Whitney was in the stands. It was a tedious start, with fifteen minutes spent languishing at the post while a colt named Aegis broke his bridle and then somehow managed to straddle the partition with his front legs. Kurtsinger even propped his feet against the side of the walls so Twenty Grand would not have to bear his weight for too long. And it was to be Twenty Grand's first start on a less-than-perfect track.

Finally, they were off. Mate rushed to the lead, and Equipoise was at sort of a disadvantage because he had started almost sideways. Always a bad starter, he got left at the post and had to scramble. Workman even said later that he considered whether he

C.V. Whitney inherited Equipoise from his father, H.P. Whitney.

With Equipoise sidelined by an injury, Twenty Grand dominated the classic year, winning the 1931 Kentucky Derby and Belmont Stakes.

should pull up and protect his colt from the pressing crowd of horses and mud. With that difficult beginning, Equipoise ran last as the field began the turn into the backstretch.

Mate was setting a brisk pace up in front, with a 1½-length lead. In the stretch, the horses began to tire of Mate's pace. Twenty Grand stayed near him. Next, Mate began to tire as well, and Kurtsinger brought Twenty Grand on, ready to close. But Equipoise came, as Estes put it, "out of the clouds in the straightaway." Equipoise pulled forward, causing the crowd to cheer wildly. On he came, with his famous chestnut coat splattered with mud. The rivals wore on, Mate just behind them, running even just

twenty yards from the wire. As they swept under it, Equipoise was in the middle a half-length ahead, while Twenty Grand stayed on the rail, beaten by half a length. Mate finished third, a scant neck behind him. The Chocolate Soldier had thrown both of his front shoes during his tremendous drive. "My greatest race?" Workman said once, when asked if the Pimlico Futurity represented his finest hour. "Hell, it may have been the greatest race anybody ever saw."

As three-year-olds, the colts first met at the Preakness, but they never reenacted their duels. Equipoise was suffering from the quarter crack that would plague him thereafter, and he took fourth place. Twenty Grand was knocked at the clubhouse turn, and this time he could not fully recover, even though he tried. Mate won the race, beating Twenty Grand by 1½ lengths.

In 1931, racing fans were accustomed to gathering around the radio to hear President Roosevelt's fireside chats, which had started in March. The Kentucky Derby, which was run after the Preakness in those days, would be broadcast, too, and people looked forward to listening as the colts took each other on. But only a few hours before Kentucky Derby post time, Equipoise was scratched because of his foot, to the great disappointment of fans who had hoped to witness the greatest matchup between the rivals to date. So the Kentucky Derby belonged to Twenty Grand, who won by four lengths and broke a seventeen-year record with a 2:01⅘ time, without the Chocolate Soldier at his heels. The rest of the 1931 season belonged to Twenty Grand. He won the Belmont and then the Dwyer. Running with a hurt back, he gave the Arlington Classic to Mate. Once rested, he won the Travers, the Saratoga Cup, and the Lawrence Realization. He won the two-mile Jockey Club Gold Cup, but at a cost. He hit his front left pastern in that race, damaging his splint bone. His four-year-old season was grim as a result. He was retired to stud at Greentree but turned out to be infertile and eventually was returned to training.

Equipoise had a successful comeback at four to be Horse of the Year, winning ten of his fourteen starts, including races such as the Arlington Gold Cup and the Delavan Handicap, in which he set a

The Payne Whitney family, from left: son John, an unidentified woman, Helen, Payne, and daughter Joan

world of record of 1:34⅖ for the mile. He reigned for a few more years, taking champion handicap male and Horse of the Year honors at five. With all this success, he was kept in training yet another year, and at six he was again champion handicap male.

But it was not until 1935 that the now seven-year-old rivals met again, this time out West, wooed by a purse of $100,000 for a handicap at Santa Anita, southern California's new track. They first met at the Oakwood Handicap, where Equipoise came in first but was then disqualified after he bumped Twenty Grand as the horses were coming off of the final turn. So Twenty Grand was listed as the winner, but the beloved "Ekky" was seen as the true victor.

The furor the Oakwood created was a perfect setting for the days before the first Santa Anita Handicap. It seemed as if racing's most famous rivals would perform their traditional battle at Santa Anita, and glamour attended the day of the big race. The crowd was the largest in California racing's history and invited comparisons to Churchill Downs on Kentucky Derby Day, with spectators toting camp stools to stand on and take in the action. Bing Crosby was there, as were Mae West (she bet on Equipoise), Al Jolson, and Fred Astaire. The race turned out to be more of a sad parade for has-beens than an exciting inaugural, though. For one thing, both Twenty Grand and Equipoise were almost scratched. Equipoise acted up at the post and never really got in the race. Neither did Twenty Grand. An ex-steeplechaser named Azucar won, and Equipoise finished seventh with Twenty Grand taking tenth place.

After the California debacle, Equipoise was sent to Kentucky to stud. Twenty Grand was sent to England to race, to no avail. He came home to America and eventually lived out his retirement years at Greentree Farm in Kentucky. He died in 1948.

Equipoise's reputation remained strongest of the rivals, both among breeders and in the popular memory. In the 1950 musical *Guys and Dolls*, which focused on some hard-luck Depression characters, one of the horseplayers sings about his pick for the day: "And just a minute boys, I got the feedbox noise/ It says the great-grandfather was Equipoise." The Chocolate Soldier was a fixture forever. He was not to have a very large impact on future generations, siring only four foal crops before dying in 1938. He was, however, the leading sire of 1942, with Shut Out his highest earner. (Ironically, Shut Out was owned by Greentree, the home stable of Twenty Grand.) Equipoise was also the great-grandsire of the classic winner Carry Back.

Both horses, in the end, left a greater legacy than foal crops could convey. They left behind a memory of the best of Depression-era racing, providing the kind of excitement that a downhearted country needed, and that only two colts, racing neck and neck, straining with every stride to be the best of all, could give. As Estes' poem went:

"I remember them both in the post parade/ The bay and the chestnut, the picture they made — And how they shot from the starting gate/And scudded down the backstretch straight/ Prodigal wasters of speed."

The Great
Match Race

Seabiscuit used his early advantage to pull away
from the lagging War Admiral in the stretch.

BY TRACY GANTZ

A Triple Crown sweep almost always trumps anything an older horse can do when it comes to being named Horse of the Year. Discovery had to carry freight-train weight to take the title from Triple Crown winner Omaha in 1935. Two years later Charles and Marcela Howard's gritty Seabiscuit won up and down both coasts, carrying weight that would paralyze any modern-day Thoroughbred (and terrify the trainer) and still lost Horse of the Year to Triple Crown winner War Admiral.

Red Pollard piloted Seabiscuit to many of his important victories but missed the match race with War Admiral.

Not only did War Admiral capture that year's Triple Crown, he vindicated his famous sire, Man o' War, who missed racing's most famous triple because owner Samuel D. Riddle considered the Kentucky Derby too early for a three-year-old to attempt 1¼ miles. When War Admiral went a perfect eight-for-eight at three, twice defeating his elders, Seabiscuit could have sung and tap danced for President Roosevelt at the White House and still have not won the year-end title.

Oh, Seabiscuit earned one set of accolades from a magazine called *Horse & Horseman*. However, War Admiral received tributes from *Daily Racing Form*,

and *Turf & Sport Digest*, both considered far more authoritative.

Charles Howard set out to rectify the 1937 Horse of the Year verdict in 1938. He knew it would take an actual meeting between Seabiscuit and War Admiral on the racetrack for his horse to nab the championship. What he didn't realize was how difficult that meeting would be to arrange. When it finally came together, though, at Pimlico in Maryland just two months before the end of the year, the stage was set for one of the most memorable match races in the history of the Turf.

By the beginning of 1938, Seabiscuit, now age

five, and War Admiral had established their respective reputations. They did it the way modern horses do, not only winning major events of the day, but also by carrying and/or conceding huge weights and earning big dollars. Horses no longer come close to toting 130 pounds over any distance of ground, and no twenty-first-century trainer would consider allowing his horse to run against rivals that carry twenty-five to thirty pounds less.

A little, plain bay of modest pedigree, Seabiscuit in 1937 carried 130 pounds or more five times, three successfully. He missed by a nose to the mare Esposa while giving her fifteen pounds and finished third once with 132. Riddle's War Admiral, more elegant than Seabiscuit but also not a large colt, as only a three-year-old in 1937 rounded out his perfect season carrying 128 pounds while conceding nineteen to twenty-eight pounds in the Pimlico Special Handicap, then just for sophomores.

The earnings race meant even more because Seabiscuit during 1937 banked more than any other horse that season — $168,590 to War Admiral's $166,500. Howard believed that Seabiscuit might even be able to overtake Sun Beau's seemingly unreachable all-time record of $376,744.

Joe Palmer, toward the end of 1937 in *The Blood-*

Seabiscuit stretched his legs over the track at Pimlico.

War Admiral, Man o' War's best son, won the 1937 Triple Crown.

Horse magazine, noted that while two- and three-year-olds had in the past earned more in one year through rich futurities and derbies, Seabiscuit had outperformed any other handicap horse thus far in the twentieth century. "Not even such great racers as Equipoise, Sun Beau, Discovery, or Exterminator got as much in any one season," Palmer wrote.

War Admiral may have lost the earnings race of 1937, but it was the only one he lost. Never beaten that season, a Triple Crown winner, charismatic son of Man o' War, owned and bred by the same man, Sam Riddle, who campaigned that legend,

War Admiral had Seabiscuit surrounded. Was it any wonder that the public began clamoring for a match between the two as soon as 1938 rolled around?

The first tantalizing whiff of a meeting between Seabiscuit and War Admiral had emerged in the fall of 1937, when both were stabled at Laurel racetrack in Maryland and eligible to the October 30 Washington Handicap at 1¼ miles. The Laurel racing secretary assigned Seabiscuit 130 pounds and 126 to War Admiral. Because scale weights called for an older horse to spot a three-year-old six pounds at that time and distance, the racing secretary essentially said that War Admiral was two pounds better than Seabiscuit.

Seabiscuit disdained the rain or the off tracks that resulted. Of his thirty-three lifetime victories, only one came over a track listed as anything but "fast," and that was on a "good" surface at Saratoga against only one horse. When the going turned to anything worse, Seabiscuit usually floundered or trainer "Silent" Tom Smith dug in his heels and refused to let his horse run.

That fall Smith kept Seabiscuit in the barn one morning because of rain, and the resulting missed work plus the threat of rain for the Washington ensured that the meeting would have to wait until the next year. Smith didn't enter Seabiscuit in the race, and War Admiral, on a good track, added the Washington to his list of exploits.

Back in the 1930s, the early days of Santa Anita's existence on the West Coast, weights for the track's signature race, the Santa Anita Handicap, came out in December of the previous year. Improving horses could receive feathery gifts of negligible assignments.

Riddle entered War Admiral in the 1938 Santa Anita Handicap at the early nomination stage, but the East Coast owner never seriously intended to ship his champion to the West. Instead, trainer George Conway, who had served as Lou Feustal's foreman when Feustal oversaw Man o' War's astounding career, sent the Admiral to Florida with Hialeah's Widener Handicap in mind. Seabiscuit, meanwhile, had returned to California for his second, and perhaps most heartbreaking, attempt at the Santa Anita Handicap.

Both horses went to the post on March 5, 1938, each carrying 130 pounds, but on opposite coasts. In the Widener, War Admiral gave Zevson twenty-six pounds and a 1½-length drubbing. In California, Seabiscuit ran afoul of the early weights. Stagehand, who had never won a race before the Santa

Pimlico Special
Purse: $15,000

6th Race Pimlico - November 1, 1948
Purse $15,000. Seabiscuit and War Admiral. Winner take all. Walk-up start by George Cassidy
1 3-16 Miles. Main Track. Track: Fast.
Net value to winner $15,000.

Horse	A	Wgt	Med	Eqp	Odds	PP	St	1/2	3/4	1m	Str	Fin	Jockey
Seabiscuit	5	120		wb	2.20	2	1	1^1	1^n	1^h	$1^{1/2}$	1^4	G Woolf
War Admiral	4	120		w	.25	1	2	2	2	2	2	2	C Kurtsinger

Off Time: 4:04
Start: Good and slow
Equipment: w for whip; b for blinkers

Time Of Race: :23⅗ :47⅗ 1:11⅘ 1:36⅘ 1:56⅗ (new track record)
Track: Fast

Mutuel Payoffs
Seabiscuit **$6.40** **No place or show betting**

Winner: Seabiscuit, b. c. by Hard Tack—Swing On, by Whisk Broom II (Trained by T. Smith). Bred by Wheatley Stable in Ky.

Start good and slow. Won driving.
SEABISCUIT and WAR ADMIRAL broke to a walking start with SEABISCUIT being sent into immediate command under pressure and drew clear going to the first turn. He hugged the rail rounding the turn and was placed to pressure after being straightened into the back stretch. Going to the half-mile post, WAR ADMIRAL moved up strongly to drive abreast, and he made repeated bids under punishment until the stretch was reached. In the last quarter mile SEABISCUIT was lightly punished after stalling off early efforts then came out resolutely when Woolf urged his mount along at his best clip. WAR ADMIRAL, after joining SEABISCUIT at the half-mile post, failed to get to the front and fell back after reaching the stretch.
Scratched—Zab.

Owners: (2) C S Howard; (1) Glen Riddle Farm

©DAILY RACING FORM/EQUIBASE

Anita season began that year, received only a hundred pounds for the Santa Anita Handicap. By the time the race ended, Stagehand had gone from a novice to the winner of the Santa Anita Derby. "The final furlong was a bitter struggle between Seabiscuit and Stagehand," wrote *The Blood-Horse* of the 1938 Santa Anita Handicap, "both horses running straight and hard at a pace which carried them six lengths out of the field. But the 3-year-old never ceased to gain."

Seabiscuit, for the second year in a row, lost the race by a nose. Howard would have to wait an agonizing two years for the little champion to capture the race so dear to his owner's heart.

Racing executives around the country began trying to figure out how to bring War Admiral and Sea-

biscuit together. Howard and Smith preferred a match race to eliminate traffic trouble from other competitors while the canny Riddle played racetracks against each other in his effort to find the most ideal location for War Admiral and the largest purse. Finally, it began to look as if New York would be able to get the deed done.

Herbert Bayard Swope, chairman of the New York Racing Commission, initially tried boosting the purse of Belmont Park's Suburban Handicap. Howard proposed an even bigger purse, $100,000, and limiting the race to Seabiscuit and War Admiral.

Riddle dangled the idea of a two-race series, first in New York and later at Arlington Park in Chicago. New Yorkers, back then as they do today, didn't ap-

prove of playing second fiddle to anyone else. Eventually, the proposal came down to one race at Belmont on Memorial Day, May 30, for $100,000 over 1¼ miles with each horse to carry 126 pounds. "War Admiral will know he's been in a horse race, win or lose," an uncharacteristically chatty Smith told reporters when Seabiscuit arrived in New York by train from California April 25.

After a month of frenzied press coverage that would rival today's stalking of Hollywood starlets, the race fell apart. Neither horse appeared to be training well, and Howard and Smith blinked first, withdrawing Seabiscuit because of knee soreness.

Instead of a match race, War Admiral and Seabiscuit prepared to meet each other in the June 29 Massachusetts Handicap at Suffolk Downs. Again,

Smith withdrew Seabiscuit, this time at the last possible moment before the race. In some accounts, it was due to soreness in a leg, in others, because of the heavy track condition. The crowd of 70,000 not only faced the disappointment of not seeing the two horses meet but witnessed a lackluster performance by War Admiral. He finished fourth — the worst of his entire career — under 130 pounds on a lousy track.

Once Seabiscuit returned to California, it didn't really matter whether the Mass 'Cap defection was legit, despite the howling in the press. Seabiscuit went back to winning in the West while War Admiral became the darling of Saratoga in upstate New York, taking four races.

Seabiscuit's return to New York in the fall might

A weekday crowd overflowed at Pimlico to witness the much-anticipated race.

From left, Seabiscuit owner Charles Howard, jockey George Woolf, trainer Tom Smith, and Pimlico's Alfred Vanderbilt

have led to a meeting in the October 1 Jockey Club Gold Cup. But Seabiscuit finished third in the September 20 Manhattan Handicap on a muddy track, leaving the Gold Cup all to War Admiral.

In Maryland, meanwhile, Alfred G. Vanderbilt, who had raced Discovery and now served as president of Pimlico, thought he might have a chance to bring the pair together where others had failed. Having recently married a niece of Marcela Howard, Vanderbilt had entrée into the Seabiscuit camp. And since he so successfully campaigned Discovery in the East, Vanderbilt was certainly no stranger to Riddle.

Vanderbilt reconstructed the Pimlico Special into a $15,000 match race instead of a race for three-year-olds. And though he couldn't offer New York's $100,000 purse, he commissioned a two-foot silver cup to celebrate the long-awaited meeting of the two game champions. Howard and Riddle signed off on the race's specifics — November 1 at 1³⁄₁₆ miles, each horse carrying 120 pounds, and the race to be postponed to November 3 in case the track was not fast. Riddle also stipulated a walk-up start, because of War Admiral's dislike of starting gates, and the use of New York's starter, George Cassidy.

"I ran it on a weekday," Vanderbilt said in 1987,

recalling the famous race, "because I knew that on a Saturday we couldn't handle the crowd."

More than 40,000 people invaded Pimlico on that Tuesday, and millions more listened to the race on the radio, including President Roosevelt. "They were the two best horses in the country, and they hadn't met," Vanderbilt said. "You had so many newspapers in those days, and they almost all had racing writers who wrote about the horses, not the handle."

After a year of dodging and weaving, Seabiscuit and War Admiral actually stepped onto the same track for the same race. Now the question became one of tactics for jockeys Charley Kurtsinger on War Admiral and George Woolf on Seabiscuit. War Admiral tended to jump out to the lead and keep going, the competition rarely able to catch him. Seabiscuit had won his share on the lead as well as from off the pace. But Woolf, who had ridden Seabiscuit most of the year for injured regular jockey Red Pollard, knew he must take War Admiral's game to him.

Kurtsinger and Woolf had their horses so ready that it took three tries for Cassidy to get a good start. Once he did, they broke dead even. "Whipped away from the start, Seabiscuit immediately did something few believed he could do; he outran War Admiral down the stretch," wrote *The Blood-Horse*.

Seabiscuit drew off to a couple of lengths in front around the first turn and into the backstretch, but Kurtsinger and War Admiral refused to give up that easily. They battled back to even with Seabiscuit — "moved up strongly to drive abreast," as the official chart read.

As if the two horses knew the public had anticipated this face-off like none before, they barreled along as a team for about six furlongs. Whether War Admiral ever got his nose in front in the middle of the race belonged to the opinion of the viewer, as contemporary accounts differ. "[War Admiral] made repeated bids under punishment," noted the chart, which at no point of call listed War Admiral ahead of Seabiscuit. *The Blood-Horse* report, on the other hand, said that War Admiral "ran up to Seabiscuit, for a moment got his head in front."

In the stretch the long head-and-head clash finally told on War Admiral. He "fell back after reaching the stretch," said the chart, though perhaps it was Seabiscuit who widened his advantage. At the wire Seabiscuit had vanquished his foe by four lengths in a track-record 1:56⅗.

The Howards received the huge trophy and ultimately what Howard had really sought — the Horse of the Year title. "I'm too excited to talk," Howard said into a microphone after the race. "I'm sorry to beat Mr. Riddle and Mr. Conway, for they're both good sportsmen. But they were running against a little too much horse."

Seabiscuit's victory was decisive, and it would be the final word because War Admiral already had a commitment to stand at stud the following season. An injury early in 1939 would sideline Seabiscuit for a year, but he eventually got his Santa Anita Handicap in 1940 in what ended up as his final start to take him past Sun Beau's earnings record to $437,730.

Perhaps War Admiral got his revenge at stud. Seabiscuit failed miserably as a stallion while the Triple Crown winner went on to sire several champions, including the Horse of the Year filly Busher.

All the players have long since passed on, but the Pimlico Special trophy, that silver symbol of what might be the greatest match race of all time, remains on display. It sits as the centerpiece of several Seabiscuit trophies behind glass in the foyer of the California Thoroughbred Breeders Association, across the street from Santa Anita, site of some of Seabiscuit's greatest races, and across the continent from Pimlico.

Postwar Powerhouses

BY GEORGE BERNET

Armed. Stymie. Assault. Their names evoke an era when the world was beginning to recover from a decade of chaos. Their careers and stirring duels recall a time in Thoroughbred history when racing emerged from wartime restrictions and became energized by the postwar boom that lifted spirits and population levels in every corner of America.

They were trained by legends — Jimmy Jones, Hirsch Jacobs, Max Hirsch — the kind of racing men for whom the Hall of Fame was created.

And for three glorious seasons of a remarkable decade they formed the nucleus of a very special handicap corps, horses that accepted every challenge of weight and distance, that captured the imagination of an ever-growing racing public.

Championship racing in the 1940s meant handicap horses, those durable anywhere-anytime per-formers that were on the scene long enough to become superstars. And that designation included females, such as the incomparable Busher, who defeated Armed in the Washington Park Handicap to seal her Horse of the Year title in 1945.

Those first few postwar years turned out to be the end of the era when two-year-olds were seen as a pleasant diversion, and the classic races for three-year-olds were regarded as spring training for their life in the major leagues. Assault, the Triple Crown winner in 1946, did not seal his Horse of the Year title until he beat Stymie in the Pimlico Special. And even at that, he just edged out Armed in the *Daily Racing Form* voting for seasonal champions.

By the end of 1947, Armed, Stymie, and Assault had established themselves as the three best male horses in training. For three years they alternated in leading the nation in single-season purses and in career earnings. Their duels played out in handicap events across the country, even though the trio never met in the same race. Their world was rivalry-within-rivalry, with Armed as the fulcrum, and, as the record shows, the indisputable best of

Clockwise from top left, Assault, Armed, and Stymie were a powerful trio of handicap horses who vied for the world's richest horse title in the years following World War II.

the best. He beat Assault both times they met, including their match race in 1947, and defeated Stymie in all three of their duels.

The true long-running rivalry of the period was that between Stymie and Assault, who met eight times during their prime, with Assault winning five and his rival three of those encounters.

Despite his perfect record against Assault and Stymie, Armed did not win a title until 1947 in the only championship voting that existed at the time — the annual poll of *Daily Racing Form* staff members. In 1945 he finished as the runner-up in voting for top handicap horse behind Stymie, despite the fact that he thumped his rival in the Pimlico Special by six lengths. In 1946 he again had to settle for a close second as Assault rode his Triple Crown and a Pimlico Special victory to Horse of the Year honors.

It was that narrow defeat in the 1946 poll — after a season when Armed had reeled off eleven wins, including ten stakes, in eighteen starts — that led directly to the match race in 1947.

Armed and Assault never met during the 1946 season, and both the Calumet Farm and King Ranch forces decided that the issue of which had the better horse should be settled on the racetrack.

In mid-1947, after some negotiation, it was decided that the two would meet at 1¼ miles for a winner-take-all purse of $100,000. The race was set for early August at Washington Park in Chicago.

But the history of American match races is replete with tragedy, disappointment, and hollow victories, and this event followed the pattern. The August match was canceled when Assault suffered a shoeing mishap after being shipped to Chicago for

Armed easily defeated a compromised Assault in a $100,000 winner-take-all race that matched the two titans of the handicap ranks.

the race. In calling off the match, owner Robert Kleberg Jr. said a nail was driven too high, and Assault was a "trifle sore."

The prospect of a match between the two stars so excited the racing public, however, that the connections of Armed and Assault were compelled to reschedule the event.

It was decided to hold the match at Belmont Park on September 27, under the same conditions agreed to previously: ten furlongs, equal weights of 126.

For a week before the race — called "the Special" — rumors flew that all was not well with Assault. On the Monday before the race, the horse came back from his workout with a splint in his left foreleg. He was treated for the problem and worked sharply on Thursday but came off the track noticeably sore. Kleberg announced on Friday, September 26, that Assault was walking soundly and that the match was still on.

After the weeklong swirl of rumors, the Westchester Racing Association, which operated the Belmont meeting, decided that discretion was the better part of profit and canceled wagering on the Special.

As it turned out, on Saturday, the sore Assault was not even a glimmer of the sound Assault, and Armed drew off at will, finishing eight lengths in front of his rival.

Ironically, September 27, 1947, was the only time in their careers that Armed, Assault, and Stymie were on the same track on the same day. In the race following the Special, Stymie finished second in the Manhattan Handicap.

Armed and Assault met once more before they faded from the scene, but both were long past their best when they ran fourth and fifth, respectively, in the Widener Handicap of 1948.

With little drama, Armed beat Stymie all three times they met. In their first career encounter at

level weights in the Pimlico Special of 1945, the Calumet star won "well in hand," with Stymie third, six lengths back. In the Dixie Handicap of 1946, Armed gave Stymie six pounds (130-124) and a 3½-length beating, earning a chart comment of "galloping" to Stymie's "no match." In the Suburban Handicap that same season, Armed gave Stymie seven pounds (130-123) and won by 2½ lengths "going away" while Stymie "closed well" to be third.

The Armed-Stymie encounters were carefully produced, directed, and choreographed by Horace Allyn "Jimmy" Jones, a shrewd manager who knew Armed's distance limitations and chose his spots wisely. Where Stymie was a true stayer, whose success rate increased dramatically with every step beyond ten furlongs, Armed could negotiate 1¼ miles and not a yard farther. Of his three races against Stymie, two came at 1³⁄₁₆ miles and one at 1¼ miles.

The real battles of the era developed between Stymie and Assault. It was a true rivalry, and it was personal. Max Hirsch would forever be linked with Stymie because through a clerical oversight, he was officially listed as the colt's breeder. He would also be known as the man who had let the world's top money-winning Thoroughbred get away in a $1,500 maiden claimer. Max Hirsch was a proud man, and beating Stymie was salve to his wounds.

Stymie and Assault were remarkably similar in talent, and the main factor in their head-to-head duels was distance. Up to 1¼ miles, Assault was the better horse, giving Stymie as much as nine pounds and a thorough beating. At eleven furlongs and beyond, however, Stymie ruled, dominating such events as the 1½-mile Manhattan and 1⅝-mile Gallant Fox handicaps while spotting his rival as much as twelve pounds.

Stymie, who raced in the name of Ethel D. Jacobs, the trainer's wife, was the champion handicap horse of 1945, despite his loss to Armed in the Pimlico

In the 1946 Dixie Handicap, Armed carried 130 pounds to a runaway victory over Stymie.

Special, and led all older runners that season with earnings of $225,375. He was retired in 1949 as the richest racehorse in history with a career total of $918,485 on a record of 35-33-28 in 131 starts. While well bred and a solid performer, Stymie went on to an indifferent career at stud. His main contribution was to fund the founding of "Stymie Manor," a breeding farm that would become the nation's leader in the 1960s under the direction of Hirsch Jacobs and his partner, Isidore Bieber.

Assault, a remarkable Texas-bred from the vast King Ranch, set an earnings record during his Triple Crown season of 1946, banking $424,195, when he briefly took the career lead from Stymie. The money mark was courtesy of the newly enriched Kentucky Derby, Preakness, and Belmont Stakes, each of which carried a purse of more than $100,000 for the first time ever. Assault, who was tried at stud in 1949 and failed, was finally retired in 1950 with

an 18-6-7 mark in forty-two races and total purses of $675,470.

Armed was the Calumet Farm money machine of 1947, when he won eleven of seventeen starts and $376,325. Of that total, $100,000 came easy — the purse of his winner-take-all match race against Assault. In early October of that year, he briefly took the career earnings title away from Stymie by winning the Sysonby Mile. Stymie regained the title as world's richest horse by winning the Gallant Fox Handicap later that month. Armed raced until the spring of 1950, finishing with a lifetime mark of $817,475 on a record of 41-20-10 in eighty-one starts.

The three trainers had similar styles, ideally suited to the animals and races of the era. Their horses came off the farm and were given brief-but-intense training sessions before the start of each new season. Once the runners had reached the desired level of fitness and the campaign had begun, they were

raced regularly to stay at peak condition. The trainers eschewed workouts between stakes engagements, preferring to run their horses in prep races up to a mile to get them ready.

Armed, a son of the Chance Shot mare Armful, was Calumet Farm-bred through and through. Like Twilight Tear, Calumet's 1944 Horse of the Year, he was from the first crop of the Bull Dog stallion Bull Lea.

Armed was foaled in 1941 and earned his Horse of the Year title in 1947, midway through the period when Warren Wright's Calumet enjoyed an embarrassment of riches. Armed was preceded by Whirlaway and Twilight Tear and followed by Citation.

Modest in stature (15 ¾ hands), with an unremarkable head he carried low through his long stride, Armed was a plain brown package whose appearance gave no hint of the weight-toting tiger he was.

In fact, his rather small stature, together with a sizeable ornery streak, convinced his handlers to geld Armed as a two-year-old, a move never taken capriciously by Calumet, the nation's foremost breeder of the period.

On the track Armed was a near-perfect racehorse within his distance limitations. In races of less than ten furlongs, he was a paragon, and at 1¼ miles he was without peer, winning eight major events at the distance in his career, carrying up to 130 pounds. Under that burden he posted a time of 2:01 flat for the 1¼ miles in the Washington Park Handicap of 1946.

Armed was celebrated for his consistency by horseplayers across America, not only for his incredible winning percentage (forty-one of eighty-one, a .506 batting average) but also for his lifetime in-the-money percentage of .877. In six seasons of meeting the best horses in the nation, he was unplaced just ten times. And he did it all in the true handicap era, when weights were earned by the horses, not negotiated by their trainers.

During the seasons of 1946, when he was just edged out of the Horse of the Year crown by Assault, and 1947, when he finally attained the highest honor, Armed ran thirty-five times and never carried less than 126 pounds. He toted 132 pounds four times, 130 pounds seventeen times, 129 pounds five times, and 128 pounds three times, and compiled a composite record of 22-8-3, a win percentage of .629, and an in-the-money average of .943. He was unplaced just twice in these two seasons.

Jimmy Jones took over as Calumet trainer in 1947, when his father, B.A. "Plain Ben" Jones, was kicked upstairs to be general manager of the mighty stable. Jimmy continued what had become the family tradition — going after the largest purses, anywhere in the country. Early in 1947 Armed chased the money on a transcontinental basis. He won the Widener on February 22 at Hialeah Park and then was put on an airplane and rushed to California to run in the Santa Anita Handicap a week later, on March 1, partly as an experiment and primarily because the Big 'Cap carried a $133,000 purse. His only poor race of the season (he finished a lackluster fifth) was blamed on the fast turnaround. However, shipped back East soon after the California race, he had two weeks to recover and won the Gulfstream Park Handicap on March 22.

Stymie, also a foal of 1941, turned into the all-American success story of riches-to-rags-to-riches.

His breeding suggests nothing but Turf royalty. By Equestrian—Stop Watch, by On Watch, he was a grandson of the immortal Equipoise, and a line-bred Domino with a cross to Man o' War. He was bred in Texas by Robert J. Kleberg Jr.'s incredibly successful King Ranch, although due to an office error, trainer Max Hirsch's name appeared on the foal papers forever.

A rich, red chestnut, Stymie had a head of striking beauty and near-perfect conformation for the distance-loving champion he became. He was

Stymie regained the title as world's richest horse and defeated Assault, who ran third, in the 1946 Gallant Fox Handicap at Jamaica.

described by some as the very beau ideal of the Cup horse.

With all that said, why did he end up in a $1,500 claiming race at Belmont Park on June 2, 1943? The answer lay in Stymie's highly individualistic personality.

He was, at best, a very difficult horse to train. Born with a mind of his own, Stymie did exactly what he wanted to do, rarely what his handlers wanted him to do. That included at times calling an abrupt halt to his morning work without warning,

much to the dismay of trainer and exercise rider. With his lack of early speed and long stride, he was also ill equipped physically to be a sprinter. When Stymie refused to train to his good looks or his high-profile breeding, Hirsch despaired of ever getting the difficult colt to the winner's circle.

In fact, Hirsch had Stymie sold privately for $500 early in the spring of 1943, before the colt ever started. The buyer handed over the money, shook Hirsch's hand, and left a happy horse owner. When he got home, his draft notice was waiting in the

Assault won the war over the distance-loving Stymie in their 1947 battles, defeating him in the Brooklyn Handicap and the Butler Handicap, above, but losing to Stymie in the two-mile Jockey Club Gold Cup.

mailbox. He marched back to the track, retrieved his money from Hirsch, and off he went to war, leaving Stymie to his fate.

Hirsch Jacobs spotted Stymie during the post parade of a race at Jamaica on May 7, Stymie's debut, and made a note of the name. After running in a maiden special on May 29, the colt was entered in a $1,500 maiden claimer at Belmont on June 2. Jacobs was there to write the claim slip. The trainer later said he had never looked at Stymie's pedigree or past performances and claimed the two-year-old on looks alone. And he always insisted that it was destiny that he and Stymie should find each other because they shared the same birthday, April 8.

Stymie's stubbornness continued to confound trainer Jacobs throughout the horse's long career.

Mornings became complicated affairs because the trainer had to arrange for enough company to keep his charge occupied. If Stymie found himself alone on the track, he would pull himself up and resolutely refuse to move. It was because of this mulish behavior that of all the 131 starts, none gave Jacobs more angst than Stymie's walkover in the 1946 Saratoga Cup.

Stymie was scheduled to have one rival in the Cup, Trymenow, but when that horse was scratched the morning of the race, Jacobs panicked and came within a dial tone of scratching Stymie, too. In a walkover, Stymie would be asked to go around the track by himself, something he would never do in the morning. Jacobs was dreading the embarrassment of watching a stubborn Stymie pull himself up

and refuse to complete the course. Of course, the horse one-upped his trainer again because when the bell rang at the start, Stymie decided it was a real race and completed the 1¾ miles in a workmanlike 3:07⅖ despite his solitude.

Stymie was always a terrible sprinter, and his first twenty-one starts as a two-year-old were all in races of six furlongs or less. So it wasn't until his fourteenth career sprint — the twelfth after Jacobs put in the claim slip — that Stymie found a field of $3,000 maidens he could trounce going three-quarters in 1:12⅕.

Routes were his forte, as he proved beyond question as an older horse, and he won stakes from nine to eighteen furlongs during his long career. However, he could also put his dynamic stretch kick to good use in shorter events, such as the Metropolitan Handicap of 1947, when he went from twelfth to

first in the final quarter of the one-mile event.

In 1945, when he wasn't able to get to the races until May 22 because of the wartime blackout that delayed the start of the season, Stymie made nineteen starts in less than five months, including four stakes appearances between November 3 and November 30. The fact that Hirsch Jacobs believed in racing racehorses can be seen by taking a glance at Stymie's seasonal totals: twenty-eight starts as a two-year-old, twenty-nine races at three, and then three seasons of nineteen, twenty, and nineteen before tailing off as an aged horse. Once, when asked why his horses ran so often, Jacobs replied, simply, "They don't make any money standing in a stall."

As fierce as their rivalry was, Jacobs and Hirsch thoroughly respected each other and delighted in the challenge when both horses were at their best. Many years after Stymie and Assault had left the scene, and at a time when both trainers were in fragile health, Jacobs invited Hirsch and a group of other trainers to his house near Belmont Park for dinner and movies. Jacobs had a large collection of 16mm stakes race films and intended to show some of the best to his guests.

However, when Hirsch accepted the invitation, Jacobs gave strict instructions to his son, John, who was manning the projector: No films were to be shown of the Stymie-Assault races. Jacobs did not want to upset or insult his old friend and rival.

Assault, despite the fact that he was a son of Kentucky Derby winner Bold Venture and a grandson of Equipoise through his dam Igual, was perfectly unremarkable in looks, temperament, and manners. He was a dull chestnut color no one could quite describe, with a body taller (15¼ hands) than it was long, and with a head most generously described as lean and intelligent.

Only when this unpretentious package ran did he become the perfect racehorse. Fully extended, Assault was nothing less than a flyer, a runner capable of extreme speed, a gifted athlete.

And the most amazing thing about Assault is he never got to show what an amazing Thoroughbred he was.

The colt was foaled March 26, 1943, at Kleberg's King Ranch in Texas. A few months later, the just-turned weanling stepped on a nail, which punctured his right front foot. The incident left the hoof malformed and shrunken, with the frog seamed and twisted. While the foot still hurt, Assault got into the habit of trying to protect it with an awkward gait. After the injury healed, the colt continued the clumsy gait, and his trainer said he looked like he would fall down anytime while walking or trotting.

Hirsch, initially dubious about ever getting Assault to train, soon discovered that the colt's stride smoothed out completely when he ran, and

the faster he went, the smoother his action became. As Assault matured, it was often noted by observers that the colt's stride was rhythmic, perfectly controlled, and on full display in the homestretch every time he raced.

Like Jacobs, Hirsch believed in racing racehorses. The trainer had Assault tune up for his three-year-old season in 1946 with a sprint victory on April 9. The colt then won the Wood Memorial on April 20, finished fourth in the muddy Derby Trial on April 30, and captured the Kentucky Derby on May 4. Four races in less than a month, which he followed by winning the Preakness on May 11, the Belmont Stakes on June 1, and the Dwyer Stakes on June 15. That made six wins — and a Triple Crown — in seven races in just less than nine weeks.

Hirsch used the same training routine throughout Assault's career. In 1949, after Assault proved infertile as a stud, the horse was put back into training in late spring. Hirsch had his eye on the Brooklyn Handicap, scheduled for July 2, and used all his well-known tactics to produce a winning horse on the given day. The tactics, of course, included what some cynics called "public workouts" — pari-mutuel races for which the intent was to win a race, though not necessarily that afternoon.

Assault's prep came in a $4,000 allowance race at Aqueduct on June 24. Despite the fact that it was his first start in sixteen months, that seven furlongs was not his best distance, and that Hirsch put up the very young Bill Boland instead of veterans Eddie Arcaro or Dave Gorman, the players were enthusiastic about the six-year-old's chances, sending him off at thirty-five cents on the dollar.

The highly impressionable Boland was given strict instructions by the master not to touch Assault with his whip at any point in the race. Hirsch insisted he do no more than hand-ride, and none too aggressively at that, no matter how close the finish. Assault forged to the front as the field rounded the far turn, and for the last quarter-mile engaged in a spirited head-and-head duel with the sometime plater Michigan III. Boland followed his instructions to the letter, never drawing his whip, never letting his emotions interfere with his mandate. Indeed, the comment on the chart of the race would, under most circumstances, be a permanent mark of shame for a professional jockey — "weak ride."

At the wire, Michigan III was an inch in front. When the photo sign came down and the numbers went up, the crowd grew ugly. Fires were started in trash cans, and there was an ominous hum of invective directed against the jockey.

Boland, rightly fearing for his life, hopped off the scale as fast as possible and was racing back to the jockeys' room when Hirsch caught his arm.

"If you had used the whip," Hirsch asked Boland, "how much would you have won by?"

"Five lengths, maybe more," the jockey answered.

Hirsch's smile lit up the tunnel. He put his arm around the jockey in a half bear-hug and said, "That's my boy!"

The record shows that Assault, this time with journeyman Gorham aboard, took the Brooklyn Handicap and its $40,600 winner's prize by nearly a length over Vulcan's Forge. It was the last stakes victory of the Triple Crown winner's glorious career.

By 1948 the equine dream team was history as the old soldiers started to fade away. That season began an inauspicious three-year end to what had been their glorious decade.

Armed lost twice to his stablemate Citation and won just once in five starts during the early winter of 1948. Assault had only two races, starting with an allowance win on February 14. The seasonal finale for both came in the Widener Handicap on February 21, when Armed finished fourth and Assault fifth. Armed went home to Calumet for a long rest, and Assault was sent back to Texas to start a stud career at King Ranch. Stymie had the best season of the three, winning four of eleven starts before breaking down in the Monmouth Handicap on July 24.

All three returned for the 1949 season, but they proved mere shadows of their championship selves. Stymie came back in an attempt to become the first millionaire in Thoroughbred history. However, in four starts he managed to add just $7,150 to his lifetime bankroll and was retired to stud after finishing second in the New York Handicap on October 1. Assault, a dud at stud, came back to win the Brooklyn but was retired again after finishing eighth in the Grey Lag Handicap on October 15. Armed managed just two allowance wins in twelve starts and was put away for the season in September after three straight losses to stablemate Coaltown.

Armed and Assault both came back for the 1950 season, as their careers ended with a whimper rather than a bang because of accumulated infirmities. Armed managed just two victories in six starts — both allowance events — and was sent home to Kentucky after winning at Gulfstream Park on March 22. Assault, who made his seasonal debut with an allowance win at Hollywood Park on November 22, bled while finishing seventh in the Hollywood Gold Cup on December 9, and was finally retired for good.

It was the end of a remarkable era.

The Iron Duo

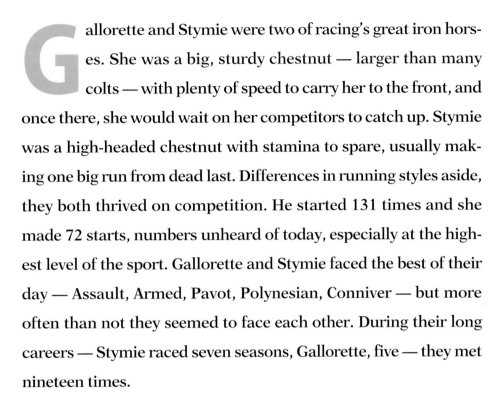

BY JUDY L. MARCHMAN

Gallorette and Stymie were two of racing's great iron horses. She was a big, sturdy chestnut — larger than many colts — with plenty of speed to carry her to the front, and once there, she would wait on her competitors to catch up. Stymie was a high-headed chestnut with stamina to spare, usually making one big run from dead last. Differences in running styles aside, they both thrived on competition. He started 131 times and she made 72 starts, numbers unheard of today, especially at the highest level of the sport. Gallorette and Stymie faced the best of their day — Assault, Armed, Pavot, Polynesian, Conniver — but more often than not they seemed to face each other. During their long careers — Stymie raced seven seasons, Gallorette, five — they met nineteen times.

Their first meeting, however, began less than auspiciously for Gallorette, who was fourth to winner Stymie in the Westchester Handicap at Jamaica on November 3, 1945. A four-year-old, Stymie had come into his own that season, while the three-year-old Gallorette was still trying to find her best form.

Bred by trainer Preston M. Burch, Gallorette was foaled in 1942 in Maryland, a daughter of Challenger II out of the Sir Gallahad III mare Gallette. Burch had acquired Gallette in 1932 along with another mare for $2,500 and put Gallette back in training for a time, although she never raced with any success. A product of William Woodward Sr.'s Belair Stud, Gallette was out of the Durbar II mare Flambette. The same year Burch purchased Gallette, the mare's half sister Flambino (by Wrack) foaled future Triple Crown winner Omaha for Belair.

With her appealing pedigree, Gallette began to receive attention from other horsemen, including W.L. Brann, who bred Challedon, Horse of the Year in

In the 1947 Queens County Handicap at Aqueduct, Gallorette scored a neck victory over archrival Stymie.

1939 and 1940, and co-owned Challedon's sire, Challenger II. Brann at first inquired about buying Gallette, but Burch suggested the two men alternate ownership of her foals. Thus, in 1941, Gallette was bred to Challenger II and the following spring, Gallorette was born, with Burch as breeder and Brann as owner. Brann undoubtedly was pleased with the deal, especially once Gallorette hit the track at two.

She was third in her debut on September 14, 1944, at Laurel Park, running over a heavy track and against males. Six days later she broke her maiden by two lengths versus fillies. In six more starts at two, she won two allowances by daylight

and placed in two others, lost the Maryland Futurity by a nose, and ran third in the Selima Stakes. She earned $7,950, all in all not a bad beginning for a Maryland-bred filly racing in her home state. The top juvenile filly that year was Busher, a daughter of War Admiral and the Bubbling Over mare Baby League. Busher had won the Selima by three lengths and had also won the Matron and the Adirondack.

The top two-year-old male that year was Pavot, a brown son of Case Ace out of Coquelicot, by Man o' War. Pavot had gone undefeated in eight starts, including victories in the United States Hotel Stakes, Saratoga Special, Grand Union Hotel Stakes, and

Gallorette often found herself in the winner's circle, even when she faced her male counterparts in the handicap division.

Stymie, shown with trainer Hirsch Jacobs, left, and owner Ethel D. Jacobs, was a frequent visitor to the Saratoga winner's circle.

the Hopeful — all traditional Saratoga stakes run at Belmont Park that year due to wartime travel restrictions.

Stymie was nowhere near the top echelon in 1944. A three-year-old, he made twenty-nine starts and won only three. Listed as bred by Max Hirsch (a paperwork delay had prevented ownership of Stymie's dam, Stop Watch, from being transferred into the King Ranch name prior to Stymie's foaling), Stymie was a son of the King Ranch stallion Equestrian. Although an unsuccessful racehorse, Equestrian did have a royal pedigree, being by Equipoise out of the Man o' War mare Frilette. Stop Watch was also out of a Man o' War mare, making Stymie inbred 3x3 to the great champion. It didn't help much in the beginning.

Stymie didn't possess much early speed and was unimpressive in his first two efforts at two, finishing seventh and eleventh while "no threat" and "no factor." Hirsch, the trainer for King Ranch, put Stymie in a $1,500 claiming race at Belmont Park on June 2, 1943. The colt ran seventh but ended up

Pavot, shown with owner Walter M. Jeffords and jockey George Woolf, posed a threat to Stymie and Gallorette.

with a new home — the barn of trainer Hirsch Jacobs. Known at the time as a claiming trainer, Jacobs probably saw Stymie as a useful sort of runner. The colt proved himself as such, starting twenty-five more times at two and twenty-nine at three and usually bringing home a paycheck. By the end of his three-year-old season, he was taking on stakes company regularly and doing well, running third in the Gallant Fox, Westchester, Riggs, and Pimlico Cup handicaps.

A wartime ban on racing halted the sport in the spring of 1945, pushing back the Kentucky Derby and Preakness Stakes until June. Pavot won the Belmont, taking the 1½-mile race by five lengths,

but he finished a dismal sixth in his next race, the Dwyer Stakes — his first meeting with Gallorette, who finished second.

Gallorette had started her three-year-old season on a winning note, taking a six-furlong allowance at Jamaica on May 22. A week later she finished second in a division of the Wood Memorial, showing she still had the ability to run with the boys. Trainer Ed Christmas sent her back to her own division, where she had no trouble taking the Acorn, Pimlico Oaks, and Delaware Oaks. From that point, Gallorette rarely would race against her own sex. She more than held her own in open company.

After her second in the Dwyer, she faced Pavot

again in the 1³⁄₁₆-mile Empire City Stakes on July 21. The colt acquitted himself much better this time, finishing second to the filly while giving her ten pounds. Gallorette was considered the top three-year-old filly in the East, as Busher was doing her running and winning on the West Coast. Pavot sputtered the rest of the year, managing placings in the Whitney and Jerome, before ending his season with a tenth place in the Lawrence Realization after stopping badly.

Gallorette too fell off form after her Empire City win, finishing unplaced in subsequent starts. Then came that inauspicious first meeting with Stymie.

Stymie had returned at four a rested and refreshed horse. He also ran like it, finishing first or second in his first eight starts. He earned his first stakes win in the June 2 Grey Lag Handicap. By November he was consistently running at the top level, having won the Saratoga Cup and finishing third in the Merchants' and Citizens' Handicap and the Jockey Club Gold Cup.

In the Westchester, Stymie showed no early speed, trailing until the field left the backstretch and entered the far turn. He then moved up steadily, wearing down three-year-old Buzfuz in the final furlong to win by a head. Gallorette had raced near the pace but just didn't have enough down the stretch and ended up fourth.

Stymie and Gallorette met again in the Pimlico Special, but the Calumet Farm four-year-old Armed, who had been first or second in all but one of his fourteen previous starts that year, ruined the party with an easy win. Stymie was third and Gallorette, fourth. It was Gallorette's final start of the year, giving her five wins in thirteen starts and $94,300 in earnings. Stymie ended his season with victories in the Riggs and Pimlico Cup handicaps. He was named champion handicap horse and earned

Stymie showed he didn't need a distance race to win when he easily bested Gallorette in the 1946 Edgemere Handicap over nine furlongs.

Gallorette narrowly defeated Stymie in the 1946 Brooklyn Handicap, the first time a female had won the prestigious race in forty years.

$225,375 with nine wins in nineteen starts.

In 1946 Stymie and Gallorette met seven times. The first encounter came in the May 4 Grey Lag Handicap at Jamaica, and the result was a repeat of the Westchester: Stymie, winner; Gallorette, fourth. Pavot, who had rebounded from his awkward three-year-old year, pushed his way into the rivalry, taking the 1¼-mile Sussex Handicap in a slow 2:04⅕. Gallorette finished second, two lengths back, and odds-on favorite Stymie, who lacked much of a pace to run at, was another length back in third.

On June 22, a week after the Sussex, Gallorette defeated Stymie again, but this time she also made it to the winner's circle, in the Brooklyn Handicap at Aqueduct.

Stymie had won the Brooklyn the previous year over Devil Diver, while in receipt of sixteen pounds. This time it was Stymie giving the weight with Gal-lorette carrying 118 pounds to his 128. Trailing early as usual, Stymie moved up on the far turn while Gallorette, who had stayed closer to the pace, moved into contention. Down the stretch it was all Gallorette and Stymie, with the filly prevailing by a neck. Third-place Burning Dream was 4½ lengths back. It was the fourth victory and second in a stakes on the year for Gallorette, who became the first filly or mare to win the Brooklyn since Tokalon in 1906. A month earlier, she had become the first filly to win the Metropolitan Handicap since Nimba in 1928.

Gallorette's jockey, Job Jessop, was understandably excited about his filly's performance: "Gallorette is the best filly I ever rode and that was the best race of her life."

After a third to Pavot in the Massachusetts Handicap, Gallorette joined with Stymie and Pavot in finishing behind Lucky Draw in the Butler Handicap.

The five-year-old lightweight (105 pounds) finished just a head in front of Gallorette (116), with Stymie (128) in third. Pavot (127) finished fifth.

The Wilson Stakes at Saratoga was an evenly matched affair, with Pavot, Gallorette, and Stymie running against Polynesian, First Fiddle, King Dorsett, and five others. At the end of the mile race, the first five finishers ended up just heads and necks apart. Pavot was the winner with Gallorette a neck back in second. Polynesian was a neck and a head back in fourth, and Stymie was another head back in fifth.

Stymie and Gallorette both entered the September 14 Edgemere Handicap, their final meeting of 1946, off victories. Gallorette had taken the Bay Shore Handicap over King Dorsett and Polynesian, and Stymie had enjoyed a walkover in the Saratoga Cup. He must have gotten something from the exer-

cise for in the Edgemere he was a decisive 1½-length winner over Gallorette.

That fall Gallorette won a division of the Beldame Stakes (only her third start against females that year) and ended her season as champion handicap mare while Stymie exchanged victories with Pavot, with Stymie taking the Manhattan Handicap and Pavot, the Jockey Club Gold Cup.

All three champions were back for more in the 1947 Metropolitan Handicap. Stymie, now six, gave his usual performance — up from dead last to finish in a rush at the wire to win. Five-year-old Gallorette had been moving strongly in the stretch before being bumped by a tiring Buzfuz but rallied for third. Pavot ended up fifth with no apparent excuses, but he came out of the race with a slight filling in an ankle. It was his final race after owner Walter Jeffords decided to retire his champion to stud rather than return him to the races in the fall.

Stymie and Gallorette soldiered on, meeting each other six more times during their busy schedules in 1947. Stymie would make nineteen starts that year; Gallorette, eighteen. In the June 2 Queens County Handicap at Aqueduct, Gallorette outlasted Stymie by a neck, and in the Butler Handicap a month and a half later, Stymie would have returned the favor if not for Assault. The 1946 Triple Crown winner was the heavy favorite and carried top weight of 135 pounds to Stymie's 126 and Gallorette's 117. The three champions finished in that order, Assault just a head in front of Stymie at the wire.

At Saratoga, Rico Monte, a five-year-old Argentinian-bred trained by Horatio Luro, snagged a couple of upsets when he took the Whitney Stakes over Gallorette and heavy favorite Stymie and the Saratoga Handicap over favored Gallorette. He had been last in the Butler earlier in the summer.

In the Aqueduct Handicap on September 1, Stymie and Gallorette were back to trading first and second place. This time, Stymie was the winner, and with the victory, he sealed his position atop the leading money earners' list with $742,210.

Gallorette was closing in on her own money title, as she attempted to best Busher as the leading female money earner. Gallorette's consistency and toughness served her well, as she placed in four more stakes that season, including a second to With Pleasure in the November 1 Scarsdale Handicap at Jamaica. Stymie, also in the race, reared at the start

then trailed as usual, leaving himself with too much to do. He finished sixth.

Through the end of her 1947 campaign, Gallorette had compiled total earnings of $351,685 in fifty-seven starts, and she finally surpassed Busher's earnings record of $334,035. Stymie's totals stood at a remarkable 115 starts and earnings of $816,060.

Both were back for more in 1948, meeting three more times. Gallorette finished in front of Stymie in two races, but Stymie got the victory when he cap-

Stymie showed his mettle when, like a gust of wind, he closed from last to catch Gallorette just before the wire in the 1947 Aqueduct Handicap.

tured his second Met Mile for his twenty-third stakes win. Gallorette was fourth. Their final meeting came in the July 17 Brooklyn Handicap. Conniver, a four-year-old Discovery filly who would go on to champion older female honors that year, upended the two iron horses with a head victory over Gallorette. Stymie hung in for third.

After the Brooklyn, Gallorette added a second Wilson score and a Whitney triumph to her tally. In early September she was sold by Brann to Marie A. Moore, who owned the 450-acre High Hope Farm in The Plains, Virginia. Moore, who had been involved with the hunting and polo set, had begun building a Thoroughbred breeding program and sought to add the well-bred Gallorette to her band of mares. The purchase price was said to be "better than $100,000."

Gallorette remained in the care of trainer Christmas and started four times for Moore, placing in the Beldame and Ladies handicaps. She was retired at the end of 1948 with twenty-one wins and thirty-three placings in seventy-two starts and $445,535 in earnings. As a broodmare she would produce stakes winners Mlle. Lorette and Courbette.

As for Stymie, in his next start after the Brooklyn, he suffered a cracked sesamoid and was sidelined the rest of the year. He returned in the fall of 1949 but started only five times, managing a second in the New York Handicap in his final start. His long, distinguished career had come to a close with thirty-five wins and sixty-one placings in an astounding 131 starts and $918,485 in earnings, a record that would stand until Citation became a millionaire.

Gallorette and Stymie faced each other nineteen times, with Stymie having the slightest edge in who had finished in front of whom the most: ten races to nine. Both had proven their worth as champion racehorses time and again but never so much as when they raced each other to the finish.

Sagamore's Sensational Fillies

Intramural rivals from the Alfred Vanderbilt barn, Bed o' Roses and Next Move finished one-two, respectively, in the 1952 Santa Margarita Handicap.

At the end of their careers in 1952, the two racemares' statistics looked remarkably alike: Bed o' Roses had won eighteen of forty-six races and earned $383,925, and Next Move had won seventeen of forty-six races and earned $398,550. It was an interesting end to a rivalry that had started when they were juveniles with Next Move acting as Bed o' Roses' "rabbit."

Theirs wasn't a traditional race-by-race rivalry. It was measured more by year-to-year accomplishments — and alternating championship titles — of these two very different fillies owned by the same stable, Alfred G. Vanderbilt's Sagamore Farm; trained by the same trainer, Bill Winfrey; and often ridden by the same jockey. In fact, when the two were coupled in the same races, their order of finish usually was determined well before they set foot on the track.

From the very start it was Bed o' Roses who had a figurative star on her stall door. Her sweet yet fiercely competitive nature endeared her to all while Next Move's stubborn and ornery disposition relegated her to a supporting role until her equal talent could no longer be denied.

Good strategy and good horses were nothing new to Sagamore Farm and the man at the helm. Born in London in 1912, Alfred Gwynne Vanderbilt was educated at Yale and earlier at St. Paul's School in New Hampshire, where he subscribed to the *Daily Racing Form* and ran a winter book on the Kentucky Derby among his schoolmates. His grandfather, Cornelius Vanderbilt II, was reputed to be the wealthiest man in the world, making his money in

railroads and shipping. His father, for whom he was named, died after giving his life jacket to a woman on the *Lusitania* when German U-boats sank the ship in the Atlantic. Vanderbilt was only three at the time. His mother, Margaret, was the daughter of the inventor of Bromo-Seltzer, Isaac Emerson, from whom he inherited Sagamore Farm.

After Emerson's death, Vanderbilt's mother had kept the stable going, knowing of her son's interest in racing.

"Since the first time I went to the races at Pimlico at the age of nine," Vanderbilt once said, "I have had this wonderful feeling about racing. I don't go to the races because I just love horses. It's like the person who goes to the circus and falls in love with the whole show, not just the elephants."

While his three marriages would come and go, his love affair with horse racing would last a lifetime. Rather than watch his horses as a society owner from a luxurious distance, he preferred to be much more hands-on both at his farm and in the industry. He became a director at Pimlico in his early twenties and was instrumental in having removed Old Hilltop, a mound for which the track was nicknamed and that obstructed the view from the stands. He soon found himself in charge of the track, adding all kinds of special events to attract patrons, including brokering a much-anticipated showdown between War Admiral and Seabiscuit in the 1938 Pimlico Special. Vanderbilt also was elected to The Jockey Club, its youngest member at twenty-four.

He was brought in to run Belmont Park in 1940. There he oversaw the installation of pari-mutuel betting in New York, where on-track bookmakers were making their last stand after being outlawed at tracks around the rest of the country.

In addition to his management skills, Vanderbilt

was an astute owner and breeder. In 1932 he had bought the two-year-old racehorse Discovery, who became one of America's best older horses, carrying up to 136 pounds, and quite a broodmare sire. Discovery sired the broodmare Good Thing, who when bred to Rosemont produced Bed o' Roses in California, where the mare had been shipped to be bred to Alibhai. Rosemont was best known for winning the 1937 Santa Anita Handicap by a nose over Seabiscuit and for upsetting the seemingly invincible Omaha in the 1935 Withers Stakes, while Good Thing was a mare of near stakes class.

Next Move also was foaled in California in 1947, her dam, Now What, having been sent there to be bred to Beau Pere later that year, after she dropped the Bull Lea foal she was expecting. Now What had

been two-year-old champion of 1939, and the exceptional Bull Lea had been the pride of Kentucky's Calumet Farm as both a racehorse and sire.

Both foals had been sent back to Sagamore Farm, and despite Next Move's sterling pedigree, it was Bed o' Roses who as a two-year-old dazzled Vanderbilt and Winfrey, who later trained Native Dancer. The talented and agreeable filly won the Matron, Selima, Marguerite, and the Demoiselle, an unheard of quadruple in the fall filly stakes, under Vanderbilt contract jockey Eric Guerin.

Next Move, meanwhile, had started her career in a maiden race, in which her obstinacy became readily apparent when she suddenly decided to stop racing, bringing up the rear by 8½ lengths. Though she showed some talent as a juvenile in

Bed o' Roses and jockey Eric Guerin joined trainer Bill Winfrey, second from right, and owner Alfred G. Vanderbilt, far right, in the Belmont Park winner's circle.

Although a taller, rangier type than Bed o' Roses, Next Move was not as effective running against males.

later minor allowance races, her secondary role to Bed o' Roses was cast.

The November 8 Demoiselle brought out Rare Perfume, a George Widener filly who had proven an able competitor with Bed o' Roses from earlier in their juvenile year. To soften up Rare Perfume, the Vanderbilt stable also had entered Next Move, who performed her role as rabbit well. She hustled her target in the race's early stages, and Bed o' Roses came on in the stretch to pass both under a hand ride. Next Move finished an easy second, five lengths ahead of Rare Perfume.

"If the race had been taken at face value [taking assigned weights into account]," wrote Joe Palmer in *American Race Horses 1950*, "Next Move was just as good as her famous stablemate, but if a man had

suggested this at the time he would have been stared at curiously, and his friends would have been wary about leaving him by himself."

This victory closed a two-year-old season for Bed o' Roses that read impressively: twenty-one starts, nine wins, three seconds, two thirds, and earnings of $199,200. Even compared with the leading money-winning colts, only Alsab ever ran more as a two-year-old, racing twenty-two times.

In fact, Bed o' Roses was selected the top two-year-old filly of 1949 with hardly a dissenting vote.

Next Move ended her two-year-old season with two victories and four placings, two of them in stakes races. She also had finished ahead of a third-place Bed o' Roses in an allowance race at Belmont Park carrying six fewer pounds (116) than her stablemate but two more than the winner, Fais Do Do.

The following year Next Move raced into the limelight, letting it be known her talent would not be squandered. Bed o' Roses, as sweet as she was, had no plans to get shoved aside. The two three-year-old fillies battled all season, though usually against different opponents.

Under the glare, the two fillies' differences became more pronounced. Next Move was a much larger, masculine-looking filly in contrast to the diminutive Bed o' Roses, who had grown little be-

In the first stakes meeting between the two stablemates, Bed o' Roses, above, won the 1949 Demoiselle Stakes over Next Move.

tween ages two and three, standing at 15 hands. There was also the issue of personality.

"Of all the good horses I've had, I think Bed o' Roses is the nicest, and Next Move is the meanest," their trainer Winfrey told race writer Bob Cooke in 1950.

Ironically, it was the sweet Bed o' Roses who did

well against the colts in 1950 while rugged Next Move struggled in male company but mowed down the competition in filly races.

Next Move finished 1950 with an impressive eleven victories in nineteen starts, going unplaced only three times and earning $240,450. Two of these weaker performances were her lone attempts against the boys. In the Wood Memorial, she finished fourth, and in the Discovery Handicap she finished fifth, beaten thirteen lengths in the worst defeat of her season. In between these two defeats, she showed herself as very capable against the ladies, winning the Coaching Club American Oaks, Delaware Oaks, and Gazelle Stakes, and later the Ladies and Beldame handicaps.

In the Gazelle, she had faced Bed o' Roses, conceding five pounds to her stablemate. Though Next Move led almost the entire way, her connections had a concession of their own — Bed o' Roses, in only her second start of the year, was being held back to protect the allowances she could get in later races. Everyone deemed Next Move's one-length victory conclusive of nothing.

"To the onlooker it seemed a shame to watch a gallant lady lag behind because a jockey was pulling at the reins," wrote racing columnist Cooke.

Cooke also noted Bed o' Roses' displeasure after the race. "Needless to say, Bed o' Roses was a comfortable second, but she hung her head as though beaten by them all. When Next Move walked into the winner's circle, Bed o' Roses looked up for a moment sadly, and then was led away."

From New York, Bed o' Roses headed to Chicago, where she finished second in the Arlington Classic by a nose to Greek Song and ahead of such husky colts as Your Host, Hawley, Lotowhite, and others. At Saratoga, she finished second in the Travers to Lights Up, with a slew of talented colts following her to the finish line. She then scored her most impressive win of the season by decisively beating the colts in the Lawrence Realization. She finished the year with five victories in twelve starts, going unplaced only four times, and earning $49,800.

In terms of earnings, Next Move had far exceeded

Bed o' Roses, but it wasn't an easy decision for some to name the former as champion three-year-old filly of 1950 given the latter's stalwart performance against the colts.

In their first race of 1951, the Santa Margarita Handicap on January 20, Bed o' Roses and Next Move, who had been saddled as highweight at 130, faced each other among a talented field of fillies and mares. For some reason the stable was more confident in Next Move, putting Guerin in the irons and riding Nick Combest on Bed o' Roses, who was second highweight at 125. It wasn't Sagamore

Next Move's only victory over males came in the 1952 Bay Shore Handicap at Aqueduct.

Farm's day. Special Touch finished first, carrying 114, beating Bewitch, at 122 pounds, by a length. Not far behind, Bed o' Roses took show honors while it was almost four lengths back to fourth-placed Next Move.

The stablemates faced each other again in the rich Maturity in early February, coupled as favorites at 9-10 even against the colts. Once again Guerin rode Next Move (121) with Combest on Bed o' Roses (110). Given the weight differential, Next Move pushed the early pace, with Bed o' Roses nicely placed. Moving up the inside, Next Move was blocked and had to be checked and taken to the outside. Bed o' Roses moved up on the leader, Great Circle (115), and seemed about

to take charge when she faltered, dropped back, and was passed by Lotowhite, who finished second to Great Circle. The filly came back lame, and X-rays taken the next day showed she had broken a coffin bone, though subsequent X-rays revealed nothing more than a bad bruise.

"Being who she was we gave her plenty of time," Vanderbilt later explained when she returned to the racetrack in late August at Saratoga for a fairly easy, six-furlong allowance race, which she won without effort.

In the Beldame at Aqueduct in September, Bed o' Roses felt the high weight (124) she had been assigned as she bore down to catch the leader, Thelma Berger, who was carrying a paltry 110

pounds. On almost even terms with a furlong to go, Bed o' Roses dropped back to finish second by two lengths. For the Ladies Handicap, she was highweight again, this time at 126, for the 1½-mile race. After a mile the Sagamore Farm filly trailed the field of fourteen. In a brilliant move she swept past her competition, but she was unable to catch Marta, under 111 pounds, who won by 1½ lengths. Bed o' Roses was able to exact revenge in the Vineland Handicap at Garden State on October 20, even under 126 pounds, in the six-furlong race, her first stakes victory of the year.

The Comely Handicap was the crowning glory of her year. Being asked to carry 127 pounds with no other entrant assigned more than 116, she came

from last to first in the 8½-furlong race and won going away from Nothirdchance (112).

Despite winning only three of her ten starts and earning a relatively meager $86,375, Bed o' Roses was named leading older female of 1951.

"Though a good many other fillies and mares topped her in earnings, it was fairly obvious that she could have spanked them silly at level weights," wrote Joe Palmer in *American Race Horses 1951*, "and it was reasonably likely that if that coffin bone had held for twelve more seconds, she would have been the leading winner of her sex for the year. As it was, she was merely the best."

Meanwhile, Next Move won only one of her races as a four-year-old. Still, Next Move also never ran that year without conceding weight to her competitors, with the single exception of Calumet Farm's standout Coaltown. And though she did not win until late in the year, she made respectable showings, running second in the Santa Anita Handicap, beaten a neck by Moonrush. She had to take a seven-month hiatus from racing when an osselet appeared after she ran in the Firenze Handicap on May 5. She ended the year by winning the Las Flores Handicap with a speedy performance over twelve other fillies and mares and six furlongs, a distance she was not overly familiar with.

The championship give-and-take between the two mares continued in 1952 with Next Move taking the honors as leading older mare, even as her ornery personality often prevailed. She finished her five-year-old season with three wins out of twelve starts and $91,825 in earnings. Some of her losses came at her own hand, wrote Palmer. Her defeats and poor races "could be charged up to her willful disposition. On occasion, when put under pressure for a strong finish, she disregarded instructions and

Next Move defeated an impressive roster of fillies in the 1952 Beldame Handicap to earn a year-end championship.

Trainer Bill Winfrey, second from left, and owner Alfred Vanderbilt, right, joined Bed o' Roses and Bill Shoemaker in the Santa Anita winner's circle after the 1952 Santa Margarita Handicap.

proceeded at her own pace with the urbanity of a mule at a country fair."

In the Gallant Fox Handicap on April 26, she was relieved of her heavy weights. But even without the excess baggage, she showed her distaste at being the only mare by dropping back to last place after a half-mile and willfully holding on to that position the rest of the race. She showed the same disregard in the Metropolitan Handicap on May 17, running in the lead for nearly three-quarters of a mile and then deciding she was done for the day, with only

Count Turf managing to finish behind her.

After Next Move came in eighth of nine in the Top Flight Handicap on June 4, Winfrey got the message she'd had enough, and he gave the lady a rest. When she came back to the races September 8 in the Bay Shore Handicap, she showed her appreciation by coming from far back in the talented field to win the seven-furlong race.

The Bay Shore served as a handy preliminary to the Beldame Handicap, for mares and fillies, the following Saturday. Next Move triumphed in the

Bay Shore over top-class male competition and then, as top weight, secured the final victory of her career with a win in the first division of the Beldame. She ran the race in the same time as the winner of the second division, Real Delight, leaving people to wonder what would have happened had they been in the same division.

As a five-year-old, Bed o' Roses ran only three times, twice with Next Move as her running mate. In her season opener, the Santa Margarita Handicap, Bed o' Roses, carrying a hefty 129 pounds and ridden this time by Willie Shoemaker, easily came from behind to gain a length advantage over Next Move, who had set the pace the whole time under a whopping 130 pounds while taking second.

Their one-two finish was ironic considering the ruckus Vanderbilt had stirred early in the week. During a sports writers' luncheon he had criticized Santa Anita's officials for not meting out severe enough punishment for bad riders and upbraided its management for spending too much time trying to make the track fast instead of safe. His com-ments drew much ire, and he was virtually invited to take his two high-stepping ladies, and his stable, elsewhere.

Vanderbilt remained at Santa Anita, and Bed o' Roses finished third in the San Antonio Handicap as the only mare in the field of eleven. In her final race she and Next Move, the only mares in the Santa Anita Handicap, were no factor. A few days later Bed o' Roses came down with a fever. Though she stayed with the training stable until later that year, she never raced again.

Instead she was sent home to Sagamore Farm in Maryland, where she was booked to Count Fleet. With no warning, she became ill on January 5, 1953, and died almost immediately. Palmer described the loss as "incalculable, since it cut off all the generations [that] might have descended from one of the best race mares of the century."

Which begs the question, what would have happened had Bed o' Roses and Next Move belonged to separate stables? Which one would have prevailed? No doubt, it would have been a close race.

CHAPTER 8

NASHUA — SUMMER TAN
NASHUA — SWAPS

Swapping Foes

BY EDWARD L. BOWEN

Many of horse racing's greatest rivalries pit opponents against each other in a memorable match race, through a Triple Crown campaign, or over an arduous spring-to-fall season. Seldom does a horse confront two separate foes in the course of two seasons. Nashua, however, had barely rebuffed his two-year-old nemesis, Summer Tan, before confronting an even more potent challenger, Swaps, at three.

Nashua and his rivals played out their dramas as the new marvel that was television brought racing to the living room. The phenomenon of television had catapulted Native Dancer to stardom in 1952 and 1953, his distinctive coloring and rushes to victory captivating the viewing public. By the time injury cut short the Grey Ghost's career in 1954, two other colts were ready to fill his void on the television screen.

In the 1955 Kentucky Derby, Swaps led throughout and bested both Nashua, second, and Summer Tan, third, on the outside.

Nashua and Summer Tan began their rivalry as stripling two-year-olds in the spring of 1954, and a year later their battle had its climax in a dramatic one-two finish in their final Kentucky Derby prep, the Wood Memorial. Then, abruptly, Summer Tan was displaced by Swaps as Nashua's most vaunted foe.

Trained by a kindly old gentleman nicknamed "Sunny Jim," Nashua (Nasrullah—Segula, by Johnstown) came from the prototype of the traditional Eastern stable. Nashua had been bred by William Woodward Sr., whose Belair Stud had reached a pinnacle twenty-five years earlier when Gallant Fox won the Triple Crown. For much of the intervening quarter-century, Woodward and trainer Sunny Jim Fitzsimmons had enjoyed a succession of classic winners and champions, and Woodward also had become chairman of The Jockey Club.

On Woodward's death in 1953, the Belair stable was taken over by his handsome son, William Jr., who along with his glamorous wife, Ann, were prominent in society as well as in sport and business.

Summer Tan (Heliopolis—Miss Zibby, by Omaha), likewise, represented a prestigious back-

Nashua, trained by the venerable "Sunny Jim" Fitzsimmons, left, represented the rich traditions of horse racing in the East.

Swaps' performances on the West Coast fired the public's fervor for an East-West match race with Nashua.

ground. He was bred and raced in the name of Dorothy Firestone (later Mrs. John W. Galbreath) and was trained by Sherrill Ward.

In their first meeting, Nashua and Summer Tan battled first and second through the five furlongs of the Juvenile Stakes, with both taking turns in the front. Nashua prevailed by a half-length.

They next met in the Hopeful, the climactic race for the division at Saratoga's meeting, and Nashua again held sway, but only by a neck. Then, in the Cowdin Stakes, Summer Tan earned his first win in the series, drawing out to win by 1½ lengths.

The 6½-length Futurity at Belmont Park traditionally was the most important juvenile race, but only a year earlier the Garden State Stakes had been increased in prize money to more than $150,000 and was the richest race in the world.

The Futurity brought Nashua and Summer Tan together again and for the third time in four meetings, they finished lapped on each other. Nashua staved off Summer Tan on one side and Royal Coinage on the other, winning by a head.

The young duelists were unable to meet in the 1¹⁄₁₆-mile Garden State, however, for Nashua had a touch of colic. Summer Tan won by nine lengths.

In voting for the juvenile championship, Nashua prevailed, but F. E. (Jimmy) Kilroe was so impressed by Summer Tan's Garden State that he made the colt his highweight on The Jockey Club's Experimental Free Handicap. Kilroe weighted Summer Tan at 128 and Nashua at 127.

Summer Tan fell ill and was near death, so his return was delayed for several months. Nashua, meanwhile, added to the status a juvenile champion

As a juvenile, Summer Tan locked horns with Nashua in many major stakes and defeated the future champion in the 1954 Cowdin Stakes.

usually enjoys, recognition as the Derby favorite pro tem. He won both the Flamingo Stakes and Florida Derby, major preps for the Kentucky Derby. His tendency to goof about or prop during a race did not please jockey Eddie Arcaro but added a roguish charm to his television personality.

Summer Tan was finally ready to face him again in their final prep for the Derby, the Wood Memorial. Arcaro was serving a suspension, so Ted Atkinson rode Nashua. Summer Tan had the lead in the stretch and Nashua left his closing rush to the final yards before getting up to win by a short neck. Nashua was clearly the fresh prince of Belair and successor of Native Dancer as the Turf's national

television hero.

(We have a childhood memory of a daffy-acting Dodie Goodman regaling the Jack Paar show's nighttime audience with the description that Nashua would wait until the last moment and then "just stick out his chin and win." This was a cockeyed interpretation of the Wood Memorial, but, then again, they were talking about our favorite horse on big-time TV!)

Enter Swaps

The weeks between the Wood and the Derby suggested the Nashua-Summer Tan duel might give way to a Nashua-Swaps affair.

Indeed, this was to prove the case, and by the time Nashua and Swaps met in a match race that August, public interest was such that the event hit national TV broadcasts and newspaper front pages, in addition to sports reports and sports pages.

As for physical confrontations, the Nashua-Swaps rivalry offered fans great titillation but relatively little gratification. They met only twice, and it was not until after the first meeting that they were perceived as rivals at the top of the three-year-old division. That first meeting came in the Kentucky Derby, and it was after Swaps' upset of the other colt that the media would fully exploit the delicious differences in their backgrounds. There was no need for invention of the differences. The contrasts were stark and easily transfer-able from a sports mindset to other cultural and social domains.

The Swaps camp starred two Mormon cowboys, friends from Safford, Arizona, who had moved their cattle operation to Chino, California. They often wore cowboy hats and blue jeans and made a point of treating horses like the work animals they are rather than the glamorous public stars that they also can be.

Nashua, as stated, came with neither cowboy hats nor spurs as stage props. His owners' backgrounds savored of pinstripes and boardrooms.

Rex Ellsworth owned and bred Swaps, and Mesh Tenney trained the chestnut speedster. Over the years they charmed many and offended others. Tenney was said to have slept in Swaps' stall during

Nashua, center, narrowly prevailed over Summer Tan, outside, and Royal Coinage, inside, in the 1954 Futurity at Belmont Park.

Preparing themselves for the classics in the 1955 Wood Memorial, Nashua, outside, and Summer Tan continued their history of close finishes.

Derby week, for example. He did not use hotwalk-ers, but had exercise riders cool out horses under saddle. Ellsworth's ranch had no grass, and he fed horses pelleted feed, then unusual, and alfalfa hay. After Candy Spots won the Preakness Stakes in 1963, Tenney stunned Turf writers by casually hold-ing the colt's shank and hosing him down while conducting postrace interviews. The following year Tenney was photographed for *The Blood-Horse* on a Western saddle astride the high-class stakes winner Olden Times. By that time, Ellsworth and Tenney had reached the top, proving their brand of horse-manship at least as valid as more common practices on the Turf. Ellsworth was both North America's leading breeder and leading owner in earnings in 1962 and 1963, and Tenney was the leading trainer both years.

In the spring of 1955, those validations of their approach and horsemanship were for the future,

but the personality and aura of cowboys fitting in among the different traditions of style and dress on the Turf were already fascinating as Swaps started out along the Kentucky Derby trail.

While Ellsworth and Tenney prided themselves on treating a horse with low-key proficiency, the connections of Nashua approached things differ-ently. The columnist Jimmy Breslin once remarked that when Nashua was led to the paddock by two grooms and an attendant towel-man waving off flies, an observer quipped that it reminded him of the en-tourage of heavyweight champion Jack Dempsey heading to the ring. "Well, he's a nice horse and there's lots of flies around and I kind of like to treat the horse right," Fitzsimmons remarked.

Whether by use of towel-men or water hoses, Fitzsimmons and Tenney each knew how to pre-pare a Thoroughbred for supreme performances.

While ownership and training approaches created contrasts, Nashua and Swaps had similarities in the royalty of their pedigrees and in the status of their jockeys. Still, the Establishment quotient in each case came down on the side of Nashua.

Pedigree: Both colts were sons of imported stallions that were products of the illustrious European breeding operation of the Aga Khan (grandfather of the present Aga Khan). Nashua was in the first American-sired crop by Nasrullah, a high-class Nearco colt, but not a classic winner, in England; Nasrullah had been imported by A. B. "Bull" Hancock Jr., master of Claiborne Farm in Kentucky. Swaps was by Khaled, a Hyperion stallion who had been promising but likewise failed to win a classic, and whose purchase had strained the borrowing power of Rex Ellsworth. Although both Nasrullah and Khaled were products of one of the most fashionable of the world's breeding operations, Nasrullah prowled the verdant pastures of Kentucky while Khaled strolled the dusty pens of California.

Jockeys: Nashua's regular rider was Eddie Arcaro, who had won a record five Kentucky Derbys, had ridden two Triple Crown winners, and had been the nation's leading jockey in earnings five times. Swaps was ridden by Willie Shoemaker, who had youth going for him but whose distinctions of hav-

Nashua, outside, easily handled his old nemesis Summer Tan, rear, in the 1955 Kentucky Derby but found a new rival in the winner, Swaps.

ing led all riders both in earnings and wins three times still left him looking up at "the Master." Shoemaker had ridden in three Kentucky Derbys, with Invigorator's third in 1953 his best result so far. He had ridden the lukewarm favorite, Correlation, in the 1954 Derby and finished sixth.

While Nashua had starred from the spring of his juvenile season, out West, Swaps (Khaled—Iron Reward, by Beau Pere) went through a juvenile campaign that brought him to the attention of the locals as a nice kind of colt but without much national acclaim. He won a maiden race and a stakes called the June Juvenile among five races from May 20 through July 8. All came at Hollywood Park. He also placed in two other stakes. Swaps was ridden by John Burton, but the jockey was called away on a mission in his training as a Mormon, and when Swaps came back in December, Shoemaker was aboard.

A December race was technically part of his juvenile season, but in essence the launch of Swaps' three-year-old campaign. By the time of the Kentucky Derby, Swaps had won all four of his races in that period, including the Santa Anita Derby. A week before the Kentucky Derby, he impressed Churchill Downs fans with an 8½-length victory in a six-furlong event that gave him a race over the track — something Nashua did not have.

Swaps was the great hope of the California fans, who had been stung by the Derby failure of their star Your Host several years earlier. Only a year before Swaps, the West Coast-based Determine had come through for them and won the Derby, but neither he nor Your Host had been a true Californian, like Swaps.

Swaps was taken seriously, even while the Nashua-Summer Tan rivalry was still seen as paramount. Then, in the final days before the Derby, Swaps so impressed onlookers while Summer Tan was said by some to be looking like he was tailing off after his

demanding effort in the Wood Memorial. Since Summer Tan had been sick over the winter, it was easy to speculate that perhaps the Wood knocked him out.

Arcaro told Whitney Tower of *Sports Illustrated*, "I don't think we'll have as much trouble from Summer Tan as from Swaps. He's the horse to beat." Sunny Jim Fitzsimmons, in his eighties, decided not to make the trip from New York to Louisville, sending his son and assistant, John, in his stead. This led to speculation after the fact that the assistant failed to note the signs that Swaps, not Summer Tan, might be the main threat.

Perhaps out of loyalty to Fitzsimmons, Arcaro later was said to go along with the alleged scenario that he paid attention to Summer Tan for too long, and once he realized there was no threat from that quarter, it was too late to try to wear down Swaps. Nashua was favored at 6-5, but Swaps was second choice at 3-1, with Summer Tan nearly 5-1 in the ten-horse field.

Shoemaker got Swaps away and into an early lead, coming over to the rail from the number eight

The much-publicized 1955 match race between Nashua and Swaps proved to be better in theory as Nashua increased his lead throughout to win by more than six lengths.

colt Swaps was. Given Swaps' later record, it was much easier to see his Derby victory as having been achieved on merit, regardless of what strategy Arcaro might have pursued. Back in California, Swaps set about emphasizing that greatness. His four post-Derby triumphs included a bashing of the older Derby winner Determine in the Californian and a victory on grass in Chicago's American Derby.

Nashua countered with four victories of his own, as he took the Preakness, Belmont, Dwyer, and Arlington Classic. These two just had to meet again, somewhere, someday.

The Match Race

On July 20 came the announcement that Nashua and Swaps would indeed meet, in a match race, Derby distance (1¼ miles), Derby weights (126 pounds), $100,000 winner take all. The race would take place on August 31 at Washington Park in Chicago. Actor Don Ameche, a racing devotee, was often cited as having brought the parties together. Years later, however, Marje Everett, whose father, Ben Lindheimer, operated Washington Park, relayed that it was Chicago racing man Charles Wacker who introduced Woodward to Lindheimer, and Ellsworth and Tenney were already familiar with her father and appreciative of the way he had supported them prior to their becoming famous.

That differing stories on how the race was arranged would last through the years is a sidelight to the fact that conflicting ideas about the soundness of Swaps would begin almost before the colts had been cooled out.

As for the running of the race, a weekday crowd of 35,262 turned out, and it was sport that attracted them. The handle on the win-betting-only match

post. He got by with an opening quarter-mile in :23⅗. After a half-mile in :47⅖, he later recalled thinking to himself, "Well, if they just let me go a little farther like this, they'll never catch me." They allowed him the lead after six furlongs in 1:12⅖.

Arcaro had Nashua in a stalking third early, then moved to second. Summer Tan was just behind him. Leaving the backstretch, Nashua needed to get serious and he pulled nearly even. After a mile in 1:37, Swaps had plenty left, and he drew away again, or as Arcaro put it for *Sports Illustrated*, "Swoosh went Swaps."

The California-bred won by 1½ lengths in 2:01⅘. He was the first California-bred to win the Kentucky Derby since Morvich in 1922. It was to be his only race in the East that spring. While the Preakness accepted supplemental nominations, the Belmont did not at that time, so there was no chance for a Triple Crown.

The parsing of strategy about Nashua and Summer Tan and how the result might have been different reflected a lack of understanding of how great a race was less than that on all but one other race on the card.

Arcaro had scoped out the best footing on a track that was drying out unevenly after a rain. Although Swaps had set the pace in the Derby, Arcaro and Fitzsimmons discerned from their insights about match races that going to the front was the better strategy. Nashua, the 6-5 second choice, had been trained for speed, and Arcaro came out whipping and driving like it was a Quarter Horse race.

Nashua got to the preferred spot on the track and took the lead, and the 3-10 Swaps never could overcome him. Several times Shoemaker moved Swaps to challenge, but Nashua turned him back each time. The pace over the dull track was not impressive, but the effort was withering. Nashua led by only two lengths after eight furlongs, but he multiplied the margin in the final furlong, winning by 6½ lengths in 2:04⅕.

Tenney had shown his mastery in dealing with a weakness of the wall of Swaps' right forefoot through the colt's wondrous campaign. Word now came that the hoof had been bothering Swaps even before the race. In *Swaps* (Eclipse Press), author Barry Irwin cites that Ellsworth and Tenney acceded to Lindheimer's conviction that the race could not be cancelled and then warned Shoemaker's agent, Harry Silbert, not to tell the rider that anything was amiss. Shoemaker later wrote that "Swaps wasn't fit … Tenney … put a leather pad on the bad foot to protect it [for a work]. The track came up muddy after a heavy rain, and some mud got up inside the leather pad and made the infection worse."

Mrs. Everett, thinking back some forty-five years, told us that Ellsworth and Tenney had informed her father the colt had some soreness, that they were standing him in cold water, and that Nashua's owner knew about the circumstance.

Fitzsimmons had visited with Ellsworth and Ten-

ney and felt that Swaps was in top shape, and the owners of the defeated horse made either frank or brave statements such as Tenney's prepared text: "It is a well-known fact that this horse first injured his right front foot early in his three-year-old career and prior to any of his major races this year. He has been sound in every race in which he was started in 1955, including yesterday's race with Nashua."

Nonetheless, the spectacle that had seemed so grand was a race that suddenly seemed so imperfect.

Aftermath

Nashua was clearly the three-year-old champion and also was voted Horse of the Year although in his very next race he was beaten to third behind High Gun, the older champion, in the Sysonby Stakes. New York had upped the purse of that race to $100,000 in hopes of attracting a rubber meeting of Swaps and Nashua, but Swaps was consigned to the surgeon's table after the match race and did not race again at three.

Nashua concluded his campaign with a victory in the Jockey Club Gold Cup, but the unimaginable extra dose of notoriety about to envelop him stemmed from tragedy off the racetrack. Mrs. Woodward shot and killed her husband one night. The case was found to be accidental, she mistaking him for a burglar; years later the couple was the basis of Dominick Dunne's novel *The Two Mrs. Grenvilles*.

The real-life tragedy was accompanied by the parallel sports story about Nashua. Executors of the Woodward estate sold him by sealed bid, and Leslie Combs II put together a syndicate that bought him for Spendthrift Farm in Kentucky for $1,251,200. He was thus the most expensive Thoroughbred in history.

Combs announced that Nashua would race again at four and that he would stay with Fitzsimmons. Swaps came back, too, and in the winter and spring of 1956 there was thought that the rivalry might be resumed. It was destined to be restricted to press coverage and the heartfelt declarations by the respective camps. The John B. Campbell Handicap was seen as a possible venue for another meeting, and Swaps and Nashua actually both raced at Gulfstream Park in Florida, but they never again met each other.

Nashua had a good campaign, winning six of ten races, while Swaps went through an amazing year of eight wins in ten starts, liberally sprinkled with world records. Swaps then suffered a life-threatening fracture of his left hind leg. While the renowned Dr. Jacques Jenney and other veterinarians dealt with designing and applying the proper cast, it was Nashua's trainer who provided a sling he had used years before on an injured horse. Swaps survived, avoiding the dreaded laminitis that so often afflicts a noninjured limb subjected to extra weight bearing.

Swaps took his turn as Horse of the Year. At the end of the season, both were retired. Nashua had won twenty-two of thirty races and earned $1,288,565 and had supplanted Citation as the all-time leading money winner. Swaps had won nineteen of twenty-five races and earned $840,900.

Summer Tan returned as a fine handicap horse but never met Nashua again and was unable to cope with Swaps when they met.

The Nashua-Swaps rivalry was odd. It lasted from the spring of 1955 until the autumn of 1956, some eighteen months, and yet involved only two races, of which the supposed climactic one was rendered less than conclusive.

Yet, there was one overriding element that made Nashua vs. Swaps superb: They were both great racehorses.

CHAPTER 9

BOLD RULER — ROUND TABLE — GALLANT MAN

Racing's Unforgettable Trio

BY JOHN McEVOY

Fierce competition, photo finishes, and track and world records — that is the legacy of what is widely considered the best crop of three-year-olds in U.S. racing history, the class of 1957. This group included three stars eventually ranked among the best racehorses of the twentieth century by *The Blood-Horse* in the book *Thoroughbred Champions: Top 100 Racehorses of the 20th Century*. They were known during their days on the racetrack as "the Big Three" — Round Table, seventeenth on that select *Blood-Horse* list; Bold Ruler, nineteenth; and Gallant Man, thirty-sixth. All three were voted into the Hall of Fame. So were their trainers: James E. "Sunny Jim" Fitzsimmons (Bold Ruler), John A. Nerud (Gallant Man), and William Molter (Round Table).

The Big Three earned their fame the old fashioned way: by winning under high weights in record times. They combined to set or equal twenty-three track or world records (Round Table, fifteen of these; Bold Ruler, five; Gallant Man, three) and won carrying 130 pounds or more twenty-eight times (Round Table, seventeen; Bold Ruler, eight; Gallant Man, three). They didn't ring up their records running down the same airstrip, either. Those twenty-three marks came at thirteen racetracks.

The depth of the 1954 foal crop was as memorable as its quality. Indeed, like the Russian toys called matrjoschka, which contain smaller and smaller nesting dolls, the racing scene in 1957 featured rivalry among rivalry among top-class three-year-old competitors. But the major rivalry among those foals of 1954 involved Bold Ruler and Gallant Man, an equine version of the epic heavyweight boxing clashes of the 1970s involving Muhammad Ali and Joe Frazier.

Bold Ruler, who in an odds-defying coincidence was foaled on the same date (April 6, 1954) on the same farm (Claiborne) as Round Table, was a star from the start for his owner-breeder, the Wheatley

"The Big Three" of the 1957 sophomore class: from left, Gallant Man, Round Table, and Bold Ruler

Stable of Mrs. Henry Carnegie Phipps. The dark bay son of Nasrullah—Miss Disco, by Discovery, entered public life at odds of 3-2 on April 9, 1956, at old Jamaica in New York. He won that, and his next four starts, including the Youthful and Juvenile stakes, going off as the favorite in each (Bold Ruler was the favorite in all but four of his thirty-three career starts.) He finished the season with seven wins in ten starts but lost the juvenile championship to Calumet Farm's Barbizon, who in his lone stakes victory had soundly defeated Bold Ruler in the all-important Garden State Stakes. Eddie Arcaro rode Bold Ruler in five of those outings and would be his pilot in the final twenty-two races of the colt's career.

In contrast, Gallant Man's two-year-old campaign was well on the other side of auspicious, made noteworthy primarily by the odds at which he broke his maiden in his third start: nearly 50-l (he'd gone off at 31-1 and 75-1 in the first two races, getting drubbed in each). That was the first of three wins in seven starts at two, none of them stakes, for the English-bred son of Migoli—Majideh, by Mahmoud, who had been acquired by Texas oilman Ralph Lowe in a nine-horse package valued at $175,000. Gerald Bloss trained the little bay colt for most of the 1956 season before he was turned over to Nerud.

Gallant Man won his first two starts at age three, including Hialeah's Hibiscus on January 19, in which Round Table finished tenth. Gallant Man and Bold Ruler first faced each other on January 30, 1957, in the seven-furlong Bahamas Stakes at Hialeah. In this, his three-year-old debut, Bold Ruler merely equaled the track record of 1:22 in downing runner-up Gen. Duke by 4½ lengths. Gallant Man closed some ground late but was a well-beaten fourth.

Bold Ruler became as legendary as his trainer, "Sunny Jim" Fitzsimmons, left.

Nerud then shipped Gallant Man north while Fitzsimmons kept his charge in Florida, thus setting up a series of three more memorable meetings with Gen. Duke, a Calumet Farm homebred son of Bull Lea. Bold Ruler had beaten Gen. Duke while conceding twelve pounds in the Bahamas. The spread was the same for the February 16 Everglades, but not the outcome: Gen. Duke by a head over Bold Ruler. Gen. Duke's stablemate Iron Liege was a distant third.

On March 2, these three contested the Flamingo at level weights of 122. Bold Ruler prevailed by a neck over Gen. Duke in track record time of 1:47 for the nine furlongs at Hialeah. In third place came Iron Liege. The final battle involving this trio occurred on March 30 in Gulfstream Park's Florida Derby. Equaling the world record of 1:46⅘, Gen. Duke downed Bold Ruler by 1½ lengths. Both carried 122 in what was to be

Gallant Man and his trainer, John Nerud

their last meeting. The score: two wins and two seconds for each. Iron Liege finished in his now familiar third spot, another head back.

Gen. Duke made two more starts that spring, both in Kentucky, before being sidelined with a foot injury. According to retired *Daily Racing Form* columnist Joe Hirsch, this was a tremendous blow to the Calumet colt's trainer and jockey. "Ben Jones was very high on Gen. Duke," Hirsch recalled. "He considered him the best horse they'd had since Citation. Gen. Duke was a handsome individual and an extraordinary competitor. Bill Hartack, who rode him in all his twelve starts, be-

lieved he was the best of that crop."

Bold Ruler and Gallant Man resumed their rivalry at Jamaica on April 20 in the Wood Memorial. Following the Bahamas, Gallant Man had finished a good fourth in Jamaica's Swift Stakes while Bold Ruler had been engaged in his busy Florida campaign battling Gen. Duke. In a thrilling clash, Bold Ruler went to the lead at the start of the Wood, relinquished it to Gallant Man, then came back to score by a nose; both carried 126 pounds. The Wheatley colt had to produce another track mark in order to earn this victory: nine furlongs in 1:48⅘.

When they again entered the same gate, it was on

May 4 at Churchill Downs for one of the most famous renewals of the Kentucky Derby. Bold Ruler was the 6-5 favorite with both Gallant Man and Round Table at slightly under 4-1. Round Table was coming off a romping victory in Keeneland's Blue Grass Stakes, in which he set a track record of 1:47⅖. Like Gallant Man, Round Table was owned by a successful oilman who loved racing — Travis M. Kerr of Oklahoma. With Gen. Duke having suffered his career-ending foot injury, Iron Liege carried the Calumet Farm banner at 8-1.

Bold Ruler contributed little to the excitement of this eighty-third Derby, finishing fourth, out of the money for only the second time in his career. Round Table ran third. In front of them was the embattled pair of Iron Liege and Gallant Man, Bill Hartack on the former, Bill Shoemaker aboard the latter. Shoemaker misjudged the finish line, standing in his stirrups for an instant at the sixteenth pole. As Shoe admitted after the Derby, and reiterated to this writer in 1997, "No question, my mistake cost Gallant Man the race." Gallant Man lost by a nose.

Molter shipped Round Table to California, where he soon launched an eleven-race win streak. Nerud decided to pass on the Preakness Stakes with Gallant Man, sending him out instead for an impressive win in the Peter Pan at Belmont. That left Iron Liege and Bold Ruler from among the Derby principals to contest the Preakness on May 18. Making his eighth start in 138 days (he had kept on his

Round Table and his trainer, William Molter

Calumet Farm's Iron Liege spoiled the first meeting of Gallant Man, Round Table, and Bold Ruler by winning the 1957 Kentucky Derby over Gallant Man, with Round Table third, and Bold Ruler fourth.

toes with an allowance tally at Pimlico five days prior to the classic), Bold Ruler went wire-to-wire, easily besting Iron Liege by two lengths.

On June 15, Bold Ruler and Gallant Man faced off for the fourth time. Gallant Man notched the first victory of their series in dazzling fashion, abetted by his stablemate Bold Nero, who pressed Bold Ruler early. After zipping through 1¼ miles in 2:01⅖, the Wheatley colt had little left for the final two furlongs. Gallant Man swept past him before the eighth pole en route to his eight-length margin of victory while stopping the teletimer in 2:26⅗ for 1½ miles, an American record. Fatigued from his early efforts, Bold Ruler staggered in third, four lengths behind runner-up Inside Tract, beaten a total of twelve lengths.

More than three months went by before Gallant Man and Bold Ruler lined up against each other on September 28 in the Woodward Stakes at Belmont Park. Gallant Man had won all three of his starts since the Belmont, including the Travers. Bold Ruler had captured his two outings during that period, one of them the Jerome Handicap, in which he missed the track mark by a tick. But the Woodward saw these two filling the second and third spots behind the older Dedicate, who beat Gallant Man by 1½ lengths with Bold Ruler two more in arrears.

However, the terrific three-year-olds rebounded in sterling fashion. Gallant Man downed older rivals in the two-mile Jockey Club Gold Cup on October 12. Bold Ruler reeled off impressive wins in the Vosburgh, Queens County, and Benjamin Franklin handicaps, establishing a Belmont track record of 1:21⅖ under 130 pounds in the Vosburgh.

The stage was now set for the final race of 1957 involving the Big Three. Garden State Park's Trenton Handicap on November 9 was the venue. After launching his eleven-race victory skein in Califor-

nia, Round Table had extended it while competing in Chicago at Hawthorne Park and old Washington Park, and in New Jersey at Atlantic City and Garden State. His streak included two grass stakes, major among them the United Nations Handicap at the New Jersey oval. Owner Kerr was eager to again take on the dazzling duo of the East.

But like a long awaited heavyweight title fight that ends in a thirty-second knockout, the ten-furlong Trenton was relatively disappointing from the drama standpoint. Bold Ruler opened up by as much as eight lengths early over the "good" track, then sashayed home 2¼ lengths before Gallant Man. Round Table, emphasizing his career-long aversion to off going, was a dull third.

This was the last time the Big Three met, and the score read Bold Ruler, a win and a fourth; Gallant Man, two seconds; Round Table, two thirds. The Trenton served to certify Bold Ruler as three-year-old champ and Horse of the Year. Round Table was voted grass champion of 1957, Horse of the Year the next season. When he was retired after his 1959 campaign with forty-three wins from sixty-six starts, Round Table was the world's lead-

Bold Ruler won the war in the 1957 Trenton Handicap when he solidly defeated Gallant Man and Round Table.

ing money winner with $1,749,869. The game and consistent Gallant Man was shut out from year-end honors.

Bold Ruler and Gallant Man, however, were not finished with each other.

Two more clashes awaited them, both in the spring of 1958 at Belmont Park. Bold Ruler warmed up for this reunion with a tally in the Toboggan Handicap. Gallant Man went into the Carter 'Cap on May 30 without the benefit of a race. Under high weight of 135, Bold Ruler won convincingly as Gallant Man, under 128, closed ground to be third, beaten three lengths.

Winding up this remarkable series was the June 14 running of the Metropolitan Mile at Belmont. Again, Bold Ruler was assigned 135 while Gallant Man picked up two pounds from winning the Toboggan. There was a change in the outcome, too. Coming from well off the pace, Gallant Man charged past his front-running archrival to win by two lengths in 1:35⅗, missing the Belmont track standard by less than a second.

That made the final tally between these two dead even. In their eight meetings, each had finished in front of the other four times. Bold Ruler won four of these races, Gallant Man two. The equine version of Ali-Frazier was over. Bold Ruler wound up his career that season with a record of twenty-three wins in thirty-three starts, while Gallant Man was retired boasting fourteen tallies in his twenty-six starts.

Were their talents transferable? To a remarkable extent, just as on the racetrack, the Big Three made resounding impressions at stud. Before his death at seventeen in1971, Bold Ruler led the American sire list eight times, turning out ten champions including super horse Secretariat. BHe sired eighty-two stakes winners. Round Table, as durable off the track as on, was responsible for eighty-three; he died at age thirty-three. Gallant Man sired fifty-one stakes winners.

This was back when stallion books weren't as thick as sales catalogs, measuring a mere thirty-two to forty mares per year. Obviously, the Big Three's impact on American racing and breeding was enormous.

Timeless Travers

BY EDWARD L. BOWEN

The three-year-olds of 1962 were a high-class group, and what was most remarkable about their season was the number of great stretch duels they or-chestrated. Well before Saratoga's August congress, there had been at least five races of which one might logically have said as each unfolded: "That must be the race of the year."

Yet awaiting, in the weathered form of the old Travers Stakes, was a race that instantly was seen to have nudged its way into timelessness. Describing it for The Blood-Horse, the eloquent Dave Alexander began:

"I have seen a lot of races over a lot of years, and up to now I've always held that the most thrilling event I ever saw was Seabiscuit's score in the Santa Anita Handicap 22 years ago. That is no longer true. The most thrilling race I ever saw at any time at any track was last Saturday's Travers Stakes at Saratoga."

Locked together throughout, Jaipur, with blinkers, and Ridan fought to the wire.

Ridan and trainer LeRoy Jolley

To add even more luster to the performances of Jaipur and Ridan, the noble protagonists that day, was the fact that for each it was the third of those gripping, grinding, searching contests that distinguished the entire 1962 season.

Ridan and Jaipur both had stood out early in the foal crop of 1959. Ridan showed first. He was a strapping, quick-maturing bay with a dashing white blaze. He was a son of Nantallah—Rough Shod II, by Gold Bridge, a mating that in time was to be repeated with such compelling results as Horse of the Year Moccasin, stakes winner Lt. Stevens, and Thong, a female forebear of both Nureyev and Sadler's Wells. At the time Rough Shod II produced the first of her foals by the young Nasrullah stallion Nantallah, she was owned by Thomas Girdler,

retired president of Republic Steel. Girdler's health was failing, so he sold his bloodstock. The Nantallah colt went for $11,000 as a yearling to a partnership of Mrs. Moody Jolley, Ernest Woods, and John L. Greer. Mrs. Jolley's husband was a successful, well-established trainer, but the colt was sent to the care of their young son, LeRoy Jolley, then a sapling of promise and an eventual Hall of Famer. The rakish colt was seen to resemble the Nasrullah colt Nadir, whom the elder Jolley had trained to win the Garden State Stakes for Claiborne Farm, so the name was reversed, hence Ridan.

Ridan was one of those precocious two-year-olds that burst out of the starting gate at Hialeah for a three-furlong victory in the winter of his juvenile season and never did anything to flatter the disapproving attitudes of those against two-year-old racing. He swept spectacularly through seven races during the winter, spring, and summer before developing an enlarged splint in a foreleg and being rested. Ridan shared juvenile championship honors with Crimson Satan. The latter emerged late in the year, by which

time Sir Gaylord and Jaipur had taken turns suggesting championship form of their own. All four were back for a tumultuous second round at three.

The first of the great battles in top-level races in the winter of 1962 involved the most spectacular of the young colts, Ridan, and the rugged little champi-

Jaipur's victory in the 1962 Belmont Stakes was a first for his owner, George D. Widener.

on among the fillies, Cicada. Going 1⅛ miles in the Florida Derby, Cicada met her challenge at the furlong pole, and instead of gradually giving way, she fought back along the rail. Ridan was forced for the first of many times to reach for the depths of his awesome talent. It was male over female, but barely, a snorting nose over a demure one.

That spring another of the major three-year-old preps produced an even closer finish, originally, when Admiral's Voyage and Sunrise County finished in a dead heat in the Wood Memorial. Moreover, Admiral's Voyage already was the veteran of a great battle in a lesser race, having won the Louisiana Derby by a nose over Roman Line. Sunrise County was a quirky sort who had already been disqualified from an apparent victory over Ridan for taking the other horse wide in the Flamingo. Now, in the Wood Memorial, he was guilty of bumping and his number was taken down again.

The Kentucky Derby was one race with an emphatic margin as Decidedly won by 2¼ lengths in record time. Roman Line was second, with Ridan a neck behind him. The Preakness, though, found Decidedly wrung out and also found Ridan ready for another heated battle. This time the camera went against Ridan, as Greek Money got home by a nose. The brazen Manuel Ycaza, riding Ridan, stuck an elbow out at his opponent near the finish, a moment caught in a head-on photograph, but it was he who claimed foul against Greek Money. The stewards, not amused, left Greek Money's number up and suspended Ycaza.

The next throbbing finish of a major race among 1962's three-year-olds introduced Jaipur into the motif. Jaipur's owner, George D. Widener, was not comfortable with racing a three-year-old 1¼ miles early in May, so he had not aimed his colt for the Derby. Jaipur ran in the Preakness but was not really yet in prime shape, having had but a pair of

mile races at three, and he trailed home tenth. (Ordinarily the phrase "classic prep" means a race leading toward a classic; Jaipur's Preakness could be read as using one "classic" as a "prep" for another, Widener having a lifelong ambition to win the Belmont Stakes.)

Jaipur was a son of Nasrullah—Rare Perfume, by Eight Thirty, and he had the bull-headedness often associated with his sire. Nasrullah, nevertheless, was a great stallion and led the sire list five times. Jaipur was looked upon as perhaps his swan song when he came out at two to win the Hopeful and Cowdin. As it turned out, however, Nasrullah had one more champion, as Never Bend emerged from the last crop the stallion conceived before his death in the spring of 1959.

Eleven days after the Preakness, Jaipur appeared in the Jersey Derby, a nine-furlong event tucked in among the Triple Crown races, ten days before the Belmont Stakes. Jaipur led early and then in the stretch was challenged by the iron-tough Admiral's Voyage as well as Crimson Satan. The latter had a tendency to lug in, and he leaned over to his left, spoiling a superb event by nudging Admiral's Voyage into Jaipur. The three seemed to hit the wire together, but the camera spotted Crimson Satan in front. The film also spotted his misdemeanor, and he was moved back to third. Jaipur had a nose on Admiral's Voyage for the original second place and inherited the victory.

In the upper stretch of the 1½-mile Belmont Stakes, the Jersey Derby scenario was unfolding again, except Admiral's Voyage that time had the rail. Manuel Ycaza had replaced Larry Gilligan on Crimson Satan, and while he was more successful in combating the colt's tendency to lug in, that internecine skirmish cost Crimson Satan focus and momentum. He gradually fell back in the decisive final furlong. The great Bill Shoemaker had replaced Larry Adams on Jaipur and got him home a nose ahead of Braulio Baeza and Ad-

From an established family of the Turf, George D. Widener relished the prowess of his champion, Jaipur.

miral's Voyage. The longest of the Triple Crown races had results in the shortest of margins.

Admiral's Voyage's owner, Fred W. Hooper, had been in the game nearly twenty years. Jaipur's breeder and owner, George D. Widener, had been in the game nearly fifty. Eventually, Hooper would pass the

Charlie Hatton's phrase "closer than the paint on the fence" aptly described the 1962 Travers finish between Jaipur and Ridan.

centenarian mark and be the grand old gentleman that had the Turf's sentiment on his side. In June of 1962, however, it was Widener, the patrician chairman of The Jockey Club, whose victory was greeted with satisfaction. The Philadelphian was of the ilk of Eastern sportsmen who placed the Belmont above all other races, and, now, at last, he had won it.

After the Belmont, Jaipur turned so sour that he refused on occasion to train. Veteran trainer Bert Mulholland got the message and freshened him. When he returned nearly two months later, Jaipur had no trouble handling Crimson Satan in the Choice Stakes. The Travers came up next, 2½ weeks after the Choice.

Ridan was also pointed for the Travers, it being his

camp's ambition to quiet any thought that 1¼ miles was beyond his effective tether. Moreover, his splint had kept him from any of the climactic New York races the previous year, so he had yet to prove himself on that circuit. Following the Preakness, Ridan had returned to the scene of his biggest wins at two, Chicago. He won by seven lengths in the Arlington Classic but was upset by Black Sheep in the American Derby two weeks before the Travers.

Seven lined up for the ninety-third Travers, which in recent years had been revived to the sort of prestige it had enjoyed over most of its history. The filly Cicada was back to try again, under 118 pounds to 126 on Ridan and Jaipur. The knowledge rather than guess that Jaipur could handle the distance was in part responsible for his being a strong choice of the 26,000-plus, at only slightly more than 3-5. Ridan went off at a little over 5-2.

Ridan broke from the inside, Jaipur right beside him. They quickly distanced themselves from the others. Thus commenced a two-horse race in a seven-horse field, although 23-1 Military Plume came along under his 114 pounds to get to within a length in third — and become the answer to a trivia question.

As *The Blood-Horse*'s Alexander described it:

"It was a two-horse duel from the moment that Jaipur and Ridan, two of the handsomest Thoroughbreds of our time, came plunging out the stalls side by side. They were side by side and well in front of the others for all of the mile and a quarter, and they were nose to nose at the finish …

"The duel was clean and true. Neither had an excuse nor needed one … There never was more than a neck, a head, a nose between them. Willie Shoemaker was trying desperately to rate Jaipur, but his horse was hell-bent-for-running on this afternoon and even so great a reinsman as The Shoe had trouble restraining him.

"Ridan [Ycaza up] never quit. It seemed to me that he came to the lead again 20 yards from the finish, and it was here that Jaipur, which had kept his lead in front from the quarter-pole, proved his greatness and that Shoemaker demonstrated his remarkable

Travers Stakes
Purse: $75,000 Added

6th Race Saratoga - August 18, 1962
Purse $75,000 added. Three-year-olds. 1 1-4 Miles. Main Track. Track: Fast.
Value of race, $82,650. Value to winner $53,722.50; second, $16,530; third, $8,265; fourth, $4,132.50. Mutuel pool $269,335.

P#	Horse	A	Wgt	Med	Eqp	Odds	PP	1/4	1/2	3/4	1m	Str	Fin	Jockey
2	Jaipur	3	126		b	.65	2	2^{5}	2^{5}	2^{2}	1^{h}	1^{h}	1no	W Shoemaker
1	Ridan	3	126			2.65	1	$1^{1/2}$	1^{h}	1^{h}	$2^{1 1/2}$	2^{2}	2^{1}	M Ycaza
4	Military Plume	3	114		b	23.30	4	7	7	7	7	4^{h}	$3^{3/4}$	J Sellers
7	Smart	3	114			a-6.30	7	4^{1}	5^{1}	5^{h}	4^{h}	5^{2}	4^{2}	P J Bailey
3	Cyane	3	120			a-6.30	3	$3^{1/2}$	3^{h}	$3^{1/2}$	3^{2}	3^{h}	5^{2}	E Nelson
6	Flying Johnnie	3	114		b	27.15	6	6^{4}	6^{6}	6^{6}	6^{1}	7	6^{1}	C Burr
5	Cicada	3	118			10.05	5	5^{1}	4^{4}	4^{1}	5^{2}	$6^{1/2}$	7	R Ussery

a - Coupled, Smart and Cyane.

Off Time: 4:48 Eastern Daylight Time
Start: Good For All
Equipment: b for blinkers

Time Of Race: :23⅘ :47⅖ 1:11 1:35⅖ 2:01⅗ (equals track record)
Track: Fast

Mutuel Payoffs

2	**Jaipur**	**$3.30**	**$2.30**	**$2.20**
1	**Ridan**		**2.70**	**2.60**
4	**Military Plume**			**3.00**

Winner: Jaipur, dk. b. c. by Nasrullah—Rare Perfume, by Eight Thirty (Trained by W. F. Mulholland).
Bred by Erdenheim Farms Co. in Ky.

Start good. Won driving.
JAIPUR raced on even terms with RIDAN from the break and they continued as a team in a torrid duel. JAIPUR, on the outside of RIDAN, had a slight lead at the quarter pole and won narrowly in a race in which neither horse gave way. RIDAN, showing brilliant speed, was unable to shake off JAIPUR while saving ground throughout. He raced courageously to the end and was beaten narrowly in a thrilling duel. MILITARY PLUME was sharply impeded at the break when CICADA rammed into him. He dropped far out of it in the early stages, but came on strongly from the five-sixteenths pole to the wire, while racing in the middle of the track. SMART, unhurried early, was going well at the end, while racing between horses. CYANE, also impeded at the start, moved up early to follow the pacemakers, while racing on the rail. He changed course in the final eighth when RIDAN came in slightly, but was tiring at the time. FLYING JOHNNIE was outrun throughout. CICADA bore in sharply immediately following the break, impeding MILITARY PLUME and CYANE. She then failed to display any speed in the running.
Scratched—Zab.

Owners: (2) G D Widener; (1) Mrs M Jolley; (4) Mrs W M Jeffords; (7) Christiana Stable; (3) Christiana Stable; (6) Jopa Stable; (5) Meadow Stable

©DAILY RACING FORM/EQUIBASE

Ridan eventually got the better of Jaipur, in the Palm Beach Handicap of 1963.

qualities as a stretch rider. Jaipur came again to take the hair's-breadth decision."

Daily Racing Form's maestro of words, Charlie Hatton, described a slightly different, although compatible, impression: "At about the eighth pole, Jaipur seemed finally to have Ridan in trouble and may have been a short neck in front, but we had seen Ridan do that before. He was only 'shifting gears.' In a trice, he was back at Jaipur's muzzle again. Both Shoemaker and Ycaza were driving for all they were worth now, while the finish pole came up to meet them. And both colts were drawing up all their resources for one last mighty effort.

"They finished right together, closer than the paint on the fence. A long silence ensued and in that interval most of the crowed seemed to think Ridan had won …"

Back to Alexander: "I happened to call Jaipur, but this may have been more prejudice than keen eyesight, for he's my favorite horse and to my mind one of the most brilliant performers the Turf has seen in decades. Ridan's race in the Travers was [also] magnificent, one of the greatest any horse has run this year. LeRoy Jolley said he was hoping to prove Ridan could go more than a mile. After the race, Moody Jolley said Ridan had proved it. He was eminently correct. The big colt ran straight and true, showed no tendency to bear out, and fought to the last inch of ground."

While debate went on before the official finish was posted, Shoemaker was thinking he had gotten it right at the wire. Young Jolley was even more certain what his fate was, commenting "I knew Jaipur beat us. I saw The Shoe drop his head down right at the finish."

Finally the order was posted: Jaipur by a nose in a race that the length of the battle, the endurance of the competitors, and the lack of rough running placed the Travers as even better than the earlier duels of that remarkable season.

The five quarter-mile segments of the Travers were recorded as follows — :23⅘, :23⅗, :23⅗, :24⅖, and :26⅕. This made for six furlongs in 1:11, a mile in 1:35⅖, and ten furlongs in 2:01⅗. The final time matched the track record set in 1946 by the older Lucky Draw under five fewer pounds. It also bettered the Travers record of 2:01⅘ set many years before by none other than Man o' War, a record that had survived the Travers victories of such standouts as Twenty Grand, Granville, Eight Thirty, Whirlaway, Native Dancer, Gallant Man, and Sword Dancer.

Alexander mused that horsemen "were still discussing it and arguing about it at the Lantern Lodge near the track at Sunday breakfast. They were discussing it in Saratoga bars and under Saratoga's elms. Folks who love racing will be discussing it a hundred years from now, I suspect, because it must go down in history books as one of the most thrilling contests the Turf has produced."

Hatton added the further compliment that neither colt after the race seemed distressed by the monumental effort. Jaipur, of course, had clinched the three-year-old championship. Nevertheless, each had two or three more starts that year, and neither won another race.

Then again, they had certainly done enough.

(The text of this chapter originally appeared in *At The Wire: Horse Racing's Greatest Moments*. **Eclipse Press © 2001)**

Hail the King

Gun Bow often challenged five-time Horse of the Year Kelso, outside, to perform at his best.

BY EDWARD L. BOWEN

Chronicles of sport are replete with many a doleful coda. Great prizefighters enter the ring once, or twice, too often. Yesterday's football titans waffle in the line-up of unfamiliar teams, in the afterthought of their careers. Great horses litter past glories with unsightly dross.

There were moments in the summer of 1964 when such unseemliness appeared to hover over the career of even one of the grandest, Kelso.

An uninspired race here, a stunning loss there, left even the most barnacled fans wondering if, alas, greatness had slipped from the seven-year-old's sinews. Few sequences in racing, or in any other sport, therefore, are as succulent in personal recall as a series of races in which the grizzled king forestalled the lusty prince in two out of their final three jousts.

Kelso's emergence as an idol and a king began late in his three-year-old form of 1960. Kelso was bred and raced by Allaire du Pont, who owned Woodstock Farm in the pleasant countryside of Maryland and raced in the name of Bohemia Stable. The horse was a son of Your Host, himself a mercurial customer who was injured so severely in a race that his very survival seemed a pipe dream. Veterinary devotion, and an admirable stance on the part of an equine insurer, transferred Your Host from a forlorn hope to an exemplar. He was never a great sire, but he was allowed his chance to survive, and when crossed with the Count Fleet mare Maid of Flight, Your Host became the unknowing co-conspirator of greatness as sire of Kelso. Maid of Flight's dam was sired by the heroic Man o' War. At the end of the twentieth century, Man o' War was reckoned the best of one hundred years, and Kelso was rated fourth — bloodlines of the equine gods.

Gelded as a two-year-old to counter an irascible nature, Kelso developed at three under trainer Carl Hanford. The most famous jockey of the time, Eddie Arcaro, signed on as Kelso's rider just as the gelding was getting good. Earlier that year the three-year-old crop's leaders had been

Bally Ache, Venetian Way, Celtic Ash, T. V. Lark, and Tompion; consequently, Arcaro had been pretty well shut out of the glamorous wins. In the rather plain-looking Kelso, however, he had found one of those pals who eventually made him less emphatic than he used to be in assessing Citation as the greatest mount of his career.

Arcaro took Kelso through five consecutive victories to end his 1960 campaign. The Jockey Club Gold Cup was among them, and Kelso was named Horse of the Year for what turned out to be merely the first of an unmatched five times. At four, Kelso swept the old New York Handicap Triple, comprising the Metropolitan, Suburban, and Brooklyn. Depending upon one's age, this sweep is either a postscript to or one of the greatest achievements in history. At the time, the Handicap Triple was the ultimate for handicap horses, and only Whisk Broom II in 1913 and Tom Fool in 1953 preceded Kelso in its domination in a single year. Like Tom Fool, Kelso completed his sweep by carrying 136 pounds in the Brooklyn.

More applicable to this narrative, Kelso in the autumn of 1961 faced contenders from the first of four three-year-old crops that would flaunt their youthful vigor with a view to bring him down. Over that

The mighty Kelso, shown with his trainer Carl Hanford, dominated racing for half of the 1960s.

Gun Bow and trainer Eddie Neloy tarnished Kelso's usually sterling performances in the 1964 Brooklyn and Woodward handicaps.

and the next three seasons, he turned back, in successive years, such worthy challengers as Derby-Preakness winner Carry Back, Belmont and Travers winner Jaipur, and the formidable Never Bend.

Bring on thy youthful pretenders, Kelso declared, and ye shall see them consigned into mine enduring shadow.

Then, in 1964, Kelso was seven and Gun Bow was not three, but four. Kelso had already had a disappointing adventure in California, so it was a time when youth seemed about to be served, but age, experience, and hardened greatness would prevail for one maximal autumn.

The dust-up began in the Brooklyn Handicap, in late July. Kelso lunged too early, banged his head on the gate, and was saved from slumping onto his haunches only by the efforts of a gate man. After the

real break came, he ran as if dazed and finished fifth, beaten fourteen lengths. Perhaps more dazing than a bump on the head was the fastest 1¼ miles in the history of New York racing, which is what Gun Bow turned in at Aqueduct that day, leading throughout and drawing off by twelve lengths. The time of 1:59 ⅗ marked the first occasion in the proud history of New York that two minutes had been bettered for ten furlongs. Whisk Broom II had set the old record of 2:00 for New York tracks in 1913. The timing accuracy of methods that produced that mark was always doubted, but its officialdom had withstood many a great runner's efforts. It had been matched by Kelso himself in the 1961 Woodward at Belmont Park and again by Beau Purple in the Brooklyn Handicap at Aqueduct in 1962.

Gun Bow was an 11-1 shot in the Brooklyn, but

he was already a star in American racing. He had been bred by a very prominent owner, Elizabeth Arden Graham, who had devoted part of the fortune earned from her cosmetics empire to establish Maine Chance Farm in Kentucky. Mrs. Graham, who had won the Kentucky Derby with Jet Pilot in 1947, stood the modestly successful Hyperion horse Gun Shot. Gun Shot begot Gun Bow when crossed with the War Admiral mare Ribbons and Bows. The colt was purchased from Mrs. Graham after his three-year-old season, along with another Gun Shot colt, Gun Boat, for $125,000. The trainer, Eddie Neloy, had been one of the many trainers fired by Mrs. Graham. The originator of Elizabeth Arden cosmetics, Mrs. Graham was noted for her frequent changes in trainer, sometimes based on the poor fellow's refusal to use her creams and salves on the horses. Neloy delighted in telling how he once had felt compelled to hide behind the front seat of an automobile when he arrived with a client at Maine Chance to look at prospective purchases and realized that the lady of the manor was at large.

In helping the Gedney Farm of Mrs. John T. Stanley and Harry Albert acquire Gun Bow, Neloy was doing himself quite a favor. Prior to the colt's sensational Brooklyn Handicap victory, Gun Bow at four had won four major races. In California, he swept through a division of the San Fernando by 5½ lengths, the Charles H. Strub Stakes by twelve, and the San Antonio by four. After a couple of defeats, he then changed coasts and won the Gulfstream Park Handicap in Florida. Gun Bow lost twice again, then was rested a couple of months, and, upon his return, was third in the Monmouth Handicap as Mongo defeated Kelso in one of those two champions' fine duels. Gun Bow carried 124 pounds to Kelso's 130 in the Monmouth, and in the Brooklyn he got in with two pounds less, whereas Kelso remained at 130.

The Brooklyn gave Gun Bow a leg up in Horse-of-the-Year mentality, which took on an unusually emotional aura that year due to Kelso's four-year grip on the honor. Anyone who dislodged the grand one would be greeted with respect, but the cheers might be begrudgingly tendered.

After the Brooklyn, Gun Bow took up 130 pounds and demolished Mongo by ten lengths at even weights in the Whitney Handicap at Saratoga and shipped to Chicago to win the Washington Handicap under 132. Kelso, meanwhile, was freshened for a month, got his head cleared, and matched the world record for 1⅛ miles in one of his few races on turf, this in an overnight race at Saratoga. On September 7, during the Labor Day weekend, Kelso and Gun Bow met again, in the 1⅛ mile Aqueduct Stakes. Allowance conditions of the event dictated 128 pounds for each.

Arcaro had retired after Kelso's second championship season, to be replaced by the seemingly obvious selection of Bill Shoemaker. Surprisingly, however, the partnership of America's greatest rider of the time and greatest horse of the time did not develop into a highly productive fit. After a number of races, Ismael "Milo" Valenzuela became Kelso's partner for the gelding's last twenty-five starts over portions of 1962, all of 1963, and then 1964. (Eventually, Valenzuela rode Kelso in thirty-five of his thirty-eight races commencing with an allowance race in August of his five-year-old season.) Walter Blum, who had hooked up with Gun Bow for his four previous races, was aboard again for the Aqueduct.

As the professional reporter and horse lover William H. Rudy recorded it for *The Blood-Horse*, "In the fifty-third start of his amazing career, Kelso the Magnificent won the $100,000-added Aqueduct and left his owner, his trainer, his jockey, and most of the millions who saw him, live or on television, limp and breathless … Kelso stalked Gun Bow, an odds-on favorite, and pressed the betting choice every step of the way. Under a drive for nine furlongs he had slowly, inch by inch, gotten to his rival, raced with him stride for stride, and then as relentlessly pulled away."

Trainer Hanford wanted Kelso to go with Gun Bow, but his charge just did not have the sheer speed to do it. Thus, Kelso was facing a five-length deficit at one point. Once Kelso had reduced it to a length, Gun Bow edged out again to a daylight spread. Never a horse to be discouraged, Kelso dug in again and finished the job, drawing even. "At the head of the stretch, Kelso had him," Rudy observed, "and everyone who knew Kelso felt that he would keep him."

Racegoers reveled in the familiar sight of Allaire du Pont, Kelso's owner, leading the great gelding into the winner's circle.

Gun Bow, shown with his breeder Elizabeth Arden Graham, proved a formidable opponent for Kelso when he raced for new owner, Gedney Farm.

The old champion could never draw clear, but he painstakingly achieved a three-quarter-length lead at the wire. The time of 1:48 ⅗ was only two-fifths of a second outside Cicada's record for the distance at the new (five-year-old) Aqueduct.

The crowd of 65,000 had relented to what it accepted as reality. Collectively, that assemblage had made Gun Bow 1-2 and Kelso more than 2-1, but the prolonged and profound cheering of the result indicated there would be a great many tickets discarded without rancor. This was New York, Kelso territory, and over five years an affair to remember had withstood the test of true love.

The eloquent Rudy shared in that love, but he also understood nature. His report on the Aqueduct waxed both exultant and submissive: "Riders in the jockey room were excited and they pounded Ismael Valenzuela on the back. Trainers were excited, this race having been as good as they come." Then, a few paragraphs later, Rudy admitted that, "In fiction, the story can end with the old and bloody champ still the champion, but in reality the day comes when he has met his match. Happily, that day is not here yet, and when it does come, 65,066 people can say they saw Kelso win the 1964 Aqueduct and hold off the inevitable."

A month after the race "as good as they come," Kelso and Gun Bow put on a better one.

This was the 1¼ mile Woodward Stakes, run on October 3. The weight-for-age conditions of the Woodward put 126 on both Gun Bow and Kelso, and 121 on the three-year-old Quadrangle, winner of the Belmont Stakes and Travers. The field was small, only five showing up, but this was hardly an occasion when even the most gambling-oriented customer bewailed the limited wagering opportunities. Kelso was just a nickel under even money, Gun Bow a nickel under 3-2. Quadrangle was 11-2, and even the longshots were accomplished horses. The 11-1 Colorado King, from South Africa, had matched the world record for 1⅛ miles in winning the American Handicap by eight lengths that summer and had added the Hollywood Gold Cup by two and Sunset Handicap by seven. The 51-1 Guadalcanal, oddly, never won a stakes but was so reliable in placing in top company that he became one of the leading sons of the great Citation.

Walter Blum put Gun Bow on the lead early, but this time, Kelso was able to keep the margin from growing beyond 1½ lengths. At the head of the stretch, the veteran had come virtually to even terms again. Trainer Neloy had cut the holes in Gun Bow's blinkers a bit larger, and perhaps the Gedney Farm colt could see his slavering rival more clearly. Vengeance laid nearly a quarter-mile ahead, with combat inherent in every yard.

Again, Rudy rose to the timbre of his subject: "At

the head of the stretch, Kelso and Gun Bow were heads apart and stride for stride. Through the gripping last quarter-mile there was contact three times as they strained for the lead. Neither faltered. In one sense, neither came again, for each came again, with each stride. Head up, he had a narrow lead; head down, his rival edged him. At the finish, no one could tell. The eye is not that quick, and in the days before the camera finish the decision of the three placing judges could have gone either way. Out of deference to two gallant horses, judges justifiably might have called it a dead heat.

"There was a delay of some minutes, Ismael Valenzuela and Walter Blum sitting their mounts near the winner's circle, eyes on the infield board. Eddie Neloy, Gun Bow's trainer, said later that his throat was so dry he could not speak.

" … A quick look at the official photo disclosed no margin. Only close examination showed that Gun Bow, head up, had his nose on the line, while Kelso, head down and gathering himself for the next stride, lacked an inch, or maybe less than that."

John R. Gaines, whose Gainesway Farm was then relatively new as a force in the Kentucky breeding industry, had put together a million-dollar deal to acquire Gun Bow as a future stallion. The erudite Gaines came up with a comment that exhibited the depth of his respect for the runner-up: "Kelso is a transcendent horse. With all he has accomplished over several years, he is compared with Exterminator and Man o' War. For our horse, it's like comparing, let's say, Zero Mostel with Charlie Chaplin." (Mostel was currently topical as the star of *Fiddler on the Roof*.)

So, the tiniest of pendulums had tick-tocked back in Gun Bow's favor. Yet, there was more to come.

The Jockey Club Gold Cup was still run at two miles, and Kelso had owned the race since 1960. Neloy decided he wanted no part of that, and Kelso duly celebrated his fifth triumph in the event, winning by 5½ lengths over yet another set of three-year-olds in Roman Brother and Quadrangle. A week before, Neloy had allowed Gun Bow to test his legs on grass, and he had run very gamely although beaten three-quarters of a length by Turbo Jet II in the1⅝ mile Man o' War Stakes.

When John Schapiro of Laurel Race Course in Maryland conceived his Washington, D.C., International early in the 1950s, he was dreaming of meetings of stars from many nations. As matters unfolded in 1964, the International was to be the deciding race for two domestic heroes. The calendar dictated that the Horse of the Year must be decided soon, and it was to Laurel that both Gun Bow and Kelso repaired, although grass was not the favored footing for either combatant.

If Kelso were human, he would have had license to look at the stolid Laurel grandstand and the luxuriant International Village amid the blazing autumn colors of Maryland and think, "Good God. Not this hellhole again." For Kelso had run three of his noblest races in Internationals past and had suffered three of his most galling defeats. First, in 1961, it was T. V. Lark that bested him. Then, in 1962, after he had turned back American protagonists Carry Back and Beau Purple in a sizzling duel, France's Match II came along to defeat him in a race so courageous that Valenzuela was in virtual tears afterward as he praised the intrepidness of his mount. In 1963, it was Mongo who outdueled Kelso to win the International by a half-length.

So, to rest his case for retaining his Horse of the Year status on 1½ miles of grass in Laurel's Interna-

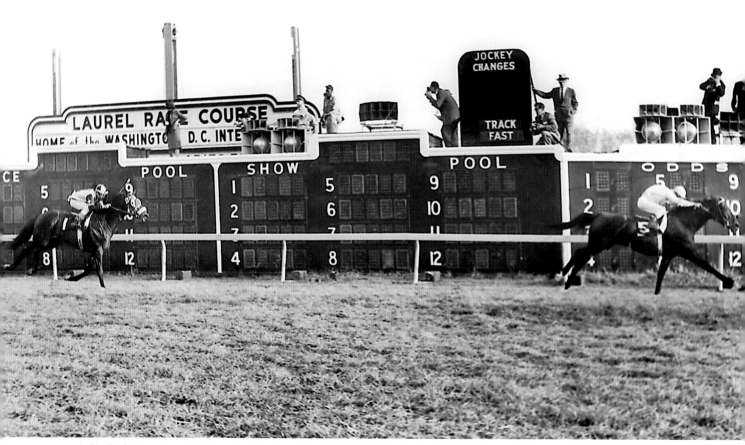

In his third attempt to win the important turf race, Kelso defeated Gun Bow in the 1964 Washington, D.C., International.

tional was hardly seen as bidding to Kelso's strong suit. On the other hand, as we have seen, Gun Bow had come up short in the only previous try on grass of his career. All in all, the International seemed readymade for one of those deflating moments when an upstart dashes home while the supposed stars struggle in feckless anticlimax.

Instead, Kelso turned it into one of his many crowning moments.

The drought-parched turf course at Laurel that autumn was far from deep, lush, or holding, and Gun Bow and Kelso scudded along as if it were the best stuff they had ever trod upon. There were some nice other runners — six of them — from Russia, Europe, and Japan, but they were never much more than curious tourists. They joined the Veteran's Day crowd of nearly 38,000 in watching a two-horse duel, and their vantage point gradually worsened.

The crowd suspected as much but not with true confidence. Kelso was favored, but only at 6-5, while Gun Bow was second choice at 3-2. Blum put Gun Bow on the lead early, and the pace was swift as Kelso tracked him three or four lengths behind through six furlongs in 1:10⅖. Valenzuela then urged Kelso toward the leader, and he reached even terms at the half-mile pole. The first mile was run in a stunning 1:34⅘. Kelso brushed Gun Bow lightly, and it took another supreme effort to begin to draw away, his powerful haunches and graceful old legs carrying with unwavering speed.

The old fellow matched the exacting standard of 2:00 for 1¼ miles again, but this time he still had two more furlongs to run. In that final stretch, he did something he had never done before — distance himself from Gun Bow. The margin and the cheers grew together, and at last Kelso had conquered the International. He hit the wire in 2:23⅘, a new course and American record for 1½ miles on grass. Gun Bow was beaten 4½ lengths, but had nine lengths on the Russian champion Aniline.

It had gone down to the last half-mile in a four-race combat totaling 5⅛ miles, but Kelso had his fifth Horse of the Year crown. Mrs. du Pont and Hanford, not for the first time that autumn, found themselves saying that this had been the most exciting of all.

Amazingly, there was more glory ahead for Kelso. His eight-year-old season did not produce a sixth Horse of the Year title, but it may not have been old legs and muscles that ended his reign. An eye infection of all things canceled most of his annual autumn schedule. Before that, however, he had put in another signature Kelso triumph when he outbattled Malicious to win the Whitney by a nose while giving him sixteen pounds at historic Saratoga. Then, in what turned out to be his final race before his New York congregation, he won the Stymie by eight lengths before the eye trouble stopped him. He made one start in Florida at nine, but the soundest of horses finally suffered an injury, a fracture in the right forefoot, and he was retired immediately.

Gun Bow won the Metropolitan Handicap in 1965 but had only two later races before his retirement, so he and Kelso did not meet again after their Laurel battle. They already had given the sport as many gifts as could be reasonably asked.

(The text of this chapter originally appeared in *At The Wire: Horse Racing's Greatest Moments*. Eclipse Press © 2001)

Substance
and
Speed

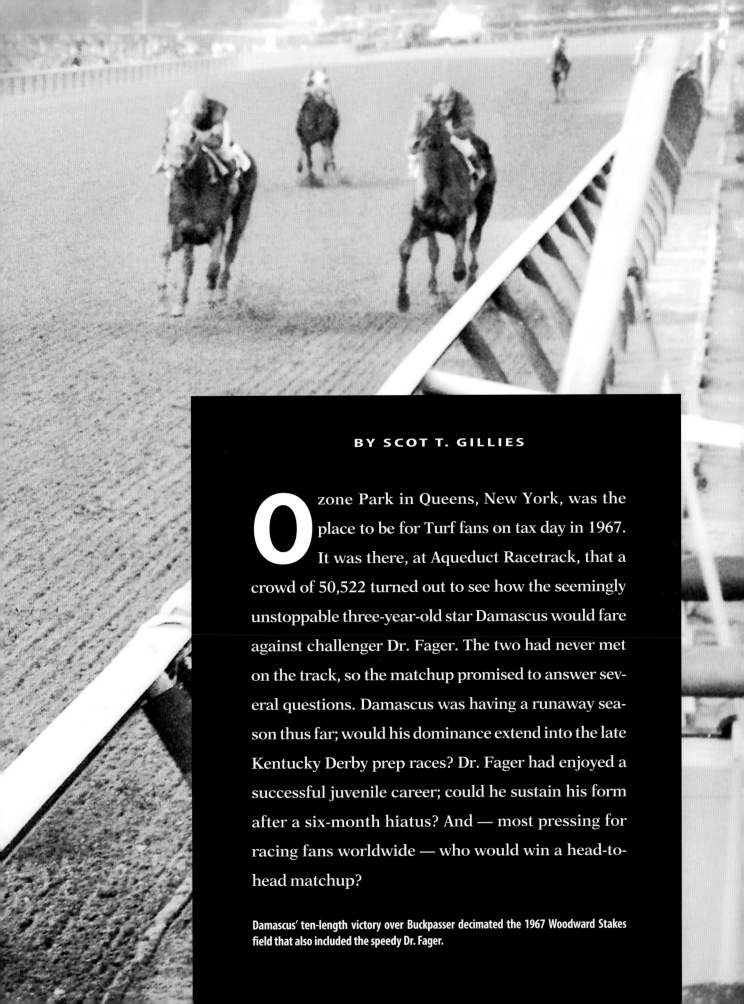

BY SCOT T. GILLIES

Ozone Park in Queens, New York, was the place to be for Turf fans on tax day in 1967. It was there, at Aqueduct Racetrack, that a crowd of 50,522 turned out to see how the seemingly unstoppable three-year-old star Damascus would fare against challenger Dr. Fager. The two had never met on the track, so the matchup promised to answer several questions. Damascus was having a runaway season thus far; would his dominance extend into the late Kentucky Derby prep races? Dr. Fager had enjoyed a successful juvenile career; could he sustain his form after a six-month hiatus? And — most pressing for racing fans worldwide — who would win a head-to-head matchup?

Damascus' ten-length victory over Buckpasser decimated the 1967 Woodward Stakes field that also included the speedy Dr. Fager.

The colts' approaches to running couldn't have been more different. Dr. Fager's take-charge running style tested the skills of his rider: A runner that cannot be rated makes controlling position and pace a difficult task for his jockey. The colt's intense, unrestrained on-track temperament seemed appropriate when considering his connections. Trainer John Nerud, the mastermind of the Tartan Farms operation, was known as a blunt, self-assured, take-charge leader who never held back when talking with reporters. His boss, stable owner and 3M Corporation president William L. McKnight, had intended to wade into the waters of racehorse ownership; Nerud convinced him to leap in with vast capital investment. Dr. Fager was one of the early Tartan homebreds, and the lanky colt's reckless technique on the track captured an audience's attention from the moment the gates sprang open.

Not so with Damascus, a strapping, sturdy colt who was content to run off the lead. Crowds watching him run grew to expect an unhurried pace until the final furlongs, when the muscular colt would exhibit a closing burst of speed that left onlookers awestruck. Damascus too appeared to reflect the character of his trainer. Frank Y. Whiteley Jr. was a respected horseman with an outwardly relaxed demeanor — so relaxed, in fact, that some Turf reporters subtly expressed uncertainty about his untailored training regimen. Damascus' dignified, confident style was equally appropriate for his owner. Edith Bancroft was the daughter of Belair Stud master William Woodward Sr., a wealthy banker whose introduction to the sport of kings came in Britain, in the company of King Edward VII and other dignitaries. Bancroft shared her father's love of racing. She was a poised and compe-

Dr. Fager proved he was a force to be reckoned with in the 1967 Gotham Stakes by handing the heralded Damascus a narrow loss.

Edith Bancroft's Damascus, shown with regular rider Bill Shoemaker, won 12 of 16 starts and Horse of the Year honors in 1967.

tent lady whose composed demeanor allowed her quietly to assume control of the Belair Stud colors following the loss of Woodward and the untimely death of her brother. The calm self-assurance displayed by homebred Damascus seemed to reflect his owner's refinement and character.

The two horses, each so different in his approach, elicited a similar excitement from race fans, and most of America had already chosen a favorite by the time the two colts finally met.

The Gotham Stakes

Nine runners went to the post April 15, 1967, for the Gotham Stakes, but expectation in the stands was that these two future Horses of the Year would easily outpace the other runners and battle each other for victory. Aqueduct's betting crowd was evenly divided between the two and made Dr. Fager and Damascus co-favorites for the one-mile contest, each carrying top weight of 122 pounds. William H. Rudy of *The Blood-Horse* wrote that the Gotham was viewed as "virtually a match race between Dr. Fager and Damascus … and that was the way it turned out."

The horses went to the gate and Damascus, with Bill Shoemaker aboard, broke quickly. The half-year since his last race as a wild two-year-old saw Dr. Fager mature considerably, and jockey Manuel Ycaza was able to rate the colt's early speed, in some measure, and in the early going they ran on the rail behind the pacesetters. Ycaza was Nerud's choice to replace Shoemaker, who had ridden Dr. Fager at the end of his juvenile campaign but who favored Damascus and had been with him in the races leading up to the Gotham.

Shoemaker and Damascus caught the leader, a speed horse that tired at the quarter pole, at the same time that Ycaza was moving Dr. Fager to the outside to challenge. On a track that was soaked by early

morning rain but holding, the co-favorites matched strides and pulled away from the rest of the field. The reddish-bay Damascus and his darker bay rival went head to head for much of the duration of the race. The two colts raced so closely that Shoemaker, riding Damascus on the inside, had to wave his crop with his left hand, not having enough room between horses to move the whip on his right side.

The bettors were justified; it appeared that the two favorites, sent out at 13-10 odds, were indeed evenly matched. But Dr. Fager was able to gain a slight advantage and managed to stick his nose, then his neck, ahead of his rival, and finished a half-length to the good in the first meeting of what was destined to be a historic series.

Shoemaker would later comment that the Gotham served as a lesson for him. "I learned how *not* to ride him," he said in frustration, accepting blame for Damascus' uncharacteristic lack of vigor in the closing strides. Having turned down the mount on Dr. Fager, Shoemaker was determined to dominate Nerud's colt when the next opportunity presented itself and brashly promised Whiteley that Damascus would never again lose to Dr. Fager if Shoemaker retained the mount.

The Kentucky Derby

In mid-April 1967, *The Blood-Horse* noted that Dr. Fager had "dead-heated" Damascus as favorites for the upcoming Kentucky Derby. A potential rematch of the two powerhouse sophomores excited the racing world and promised to make a memorable Run for the Roses.

Damascus, a son of 1959 Horse of the Year Sword Dancer, went out a week after the Gotham to capture the Wood Memorial Stakes, quite impressively, as a final preparation for the Kentucky Derby. The colt was an easy winner in a race that convinced Shoemaker his mount could handle the Derby's 1¼

John Nerud, right, trained the speedy Dr. Fager to the champion sprinter title in 1967 and to Horse of the Year honors the following year.

mile. "I feel sure he can get a distance," the jockey said at the time.

The story was different at McKnight's Tartan Farms, however, and Nerud surprised the racing world by indicating that Dr. Fager would not contest the classic races. He used the excuse of physical infirmity to keep Dr. Fager from the Derby. Asked why he wouldn't run the homebred son of Rough'n Tumble, Nerud replied, "I just don't want to. This colt has knee trouble, and I don't want to." The Thoroughbred racing establishment wondered at the time whether Nerud was afraid of a rematch against Damascus (and that suspicion seemed to be supported by Dr. Fager's entry in the Withers Stakes only a week post-Derby), but the trainer maintained his stance. Years later Nerud conceded that no serious knee problems had existed; he simply did not want to push Dr. Fager so early in his career when he worried the distance and strain of the classic race could ruin the colt.

Damascus would finish third in the Kentucky Derby, apparently unnerved by the crowd and clamor, but he won the Preakness and Belmont Stakes with authority.

The Woodward Stakes

So it was that Damascus and Dr. Fager would not meet during the Triple Crown season. Race fans still clamored for a rematch, however, and sports columnists rarely recounted the triumphs of one of the horses without lamenting the absence of the other. These appeals for a renewal of the rivalry would be answered in the autumn of the horses' three-year-old campaigns.

When the two colts went to post September 30, 1967, for the Woodward Stakes (named for the father of Damascus' owner), they had a new adversary. Buckpasser, Horse of the Year as a three-year-old the previous year, was the 8-5 betting favorite in

the $100,000-added weight-for-age stakes at Aqueduct. Dr. Fager and Damascus would start as 9-5 second-choices, with only $157 difference in "win" wagers between the two ($173,547 for Dr. Fager and $173,390 for Damascus).

Before the race even began, controversy brewed. The trainers of Buckpasser and Damascus had each entered an additional runner in the race and had been accused of sending out "rabbits" to set a fast early pace that would tire the front-running Dr. Fager. Eddie Neloy, trainer of Buckpasser, also ran the speed horse Great Power and maintained he was a legitimate entry; Whiteley responded to the charges about his own second entry by saying, "Hell, Hedevar is no rabbit" and noting that the colt was a solid runner in his own right. But Nerud was not convinced.

Reporters always knew they would get a quote — and, often, hostile treatment — when they talked to Nerud, who himself admitted, "I've got my opinions … sometimes I'd be better off if I kept my mouth shut." About the opposing trainers' rabbits, he asserted that neither had a shot at the race and they were just in it to kill Dr. Fager.

Nerud's comments struck a chord with the racing public, who were sympathetic to the trainer's frustration. Fans who had come to see the three stars face off resented the possibility that outside elements could affect the outcome; many actually jeered when Hedevar and Great Power jogged by in the post parade.

Unlike Nerud, keeping his mouth shut was exactly how rival trainer Whiteley operated, the elder horseman studiously avoiding media questions in general, and about his Hedevar entry in particular. While often unwelcoming to correspondents, Whiteley was not especially provocative when evaluating rivals; of Dr. Fager, he limited his comments to proclaiming, "I don't like to knock anyone's horse."

The much-anticipated race drew a record crowd

Dr. Fager handed Damascus, a well-beaten third, a five-length drumming in the 1968 Suburban Handicap.

of 55,259 to Aqueduct. The "Big Three" came into the race, each having been odds-on favorites in his past several outings. Dr. Fager had never finished worse than second, and Damascus was close to that record, having come in as far back as third only once, that occasion being the Derby earlier in the year.

As expected, Dr. Fager led with fast fractions and took the lead on the first turn, but by the far turn he was tiring after dueling with Hedevar. Shoemaker, again aboard Damascus, and Braulio Baeza on Buckpasser followed their scripts well and held back their mounts until the speed horses had done their jobs. Damascus and Buckpasser ran together for a half-furlong in pursuit of Dr. Fager, but Damascus

pulled ahead and outran them both. Buckpasser caught the worn Dr. Fager in the final seconds and bested him for place by a half-length, but Damascus was far away the winner. On a track that was officially "fast" — though it was called "heavy" for earlier races — Damascus came home with a final time of 2:00⅗, an Aqueduct record for the ten-furlong distance. Seemingly supporting the charge that they were entered as spoilers, Hedevar and Great Power finished last, beaten dozens of lengths. Nerud was outraged when Dr. Fager's jockey Bill Boland reported to him about the screams and shouts from the rabbits' riders that were intended to push Dr. Fager to a fatiguing early pace (though Boland himself conceded that he had engaged in similar practices when he thought it could help him win a race).

The connections of the winner were jubilant. Shoemaker, having settled the score against his old mount Dr. Fager, said of Damascus, "I guess he's as good a horse as I ever rode." The victory silenced Whiteley's critics, who thought the conditioner's training schedule was too casual to bring Damascus to top form.

Darby Dan Farm, which stood Damascus' sire, Sword Dancer, would advertise that stallion's stud services later in the year using an impressive photo of the Woodward that showed Damascus by far the best horse, approaching the finish on the far right of the photo, with Dr. Fager and Buckpasser battling for second, well on the left of the image, ten lengths of daylight behind the winner.

Damascus and Dr. Fager would not go head to

head again in 1967; they finished the season tied at one win each in the series.

Suburban Handicap

It would be more than nine months before the two champions would meet, this time as more mature four-year-olds. The physical differences in the colts had never been more apparent than when they pranced out for the post parade ahead of the eighty-second running of the Suburban Handicap on Independence Day in 1968. Dr. Fager had always been lighter bodied and long legged and now was one of the tallest horses in racing. His stature was in contrast to that of Damascus, a heavily muscled colt whose nicely proportioned conformation made him appear smaller than his actual 16-hand height.

Dr. Fager came into the race unbeaten in only two starts in 1968, having missed the Metropolitan

With a five-pound weight advantage, Damascus avenged his Suburban loss to Dr. Fager, second, in the Brooklyn Handicap.

due to a frightening bout of colic. Damascus, turned out for nearly two months earlier in the year, had come back to win an allowance race easily. Also featured in the Suburban, which was run at Aqueduct, was In Reality, another stellar four-year-old who threatened for honors as the star of the 1964 foal crop. A repeat of "rabbit" accusations was avoided when Hedevar was withdrawn shortly before the race following a minor training injury. Upon hearing the news of Hedevar's scratch, Nerud — who had protested loudly and often that the sprint horse's entry in the race was meant only to tire Dr. Fager — told anyone who would listen, "That's good — the race is over."

The Suburban being a handicap contest, Damascus and Dr. Fager were assigned rather high weights to even out the field. Damascus carried 133 pounds and Dr. Fager 132, indicative of their elite status and sensational records; the next high weight was In Reality at 125. Even with the significant weight handicap, the crowd of 54,336 sent off Dr. Fager as the 4-5 favorite, with Damascus at 7-5.

The race unfolded with each horse running in his signature style. Damascus, with Manuel Ycaza now aboard as his regular rider to replace an injured Shoemaker, broke well, but Baeza, newly inaugurated with his own mount, quickly took Dr. Fager to a short lead on the rail going into the clubhouse turn. In the backstretch Ycaza brought Damascus up alongside Dr. Fager, and the two ran stride for stride. When Damascus made a move to take control of the race, Dr. Fager matched his opponent's effort. At the five-eighths pole, Damascus nosed in front for a few strides before his rival again took the lead. The two ran together, Damascus gamely trying several times to take command, but at the beginning of the stretch Dr. Fager began to pull away.

Following the grueling contest with Damascus, Dr. Fager had no time to enjoy the lead as Bold

Hour, who carried only 116 pounds, came to challenge. Baeza had expected to see In Reality and was surprised to find another horse contesting the race; regardless, it was futile competition. Dr. Fager fought back and finished the ten furlongs in 1:59⅗, equaling the track record. Damascus finished a well-beaten third behind the light-weighted Bold Hour. Nerud, whose temper still flared at the mention of Hedevar, reflected that "there's never been a race in my life that did me as much good" as seeing Dr. Fager win a head-to-head matchup with Damascus.

Brooklyn Handicap

After waiting so long for the great rivals to clash as four-year-olds, fans of the two racehorses delighted in another contest only sixteen days after the Suburban. *The Blood-Horse* writer Rudy, who had chronicled the antagonists' careers, exclaimed in anticipation of the colts' fourth meeting, "Damascus and Dr. Fager! There is so little to choose between these so-different Thoroughbreds, each magnificent in his own way."

The stage was set, yet again at Aqueduct, for the eightieth running of the Brooklyn Handicap. Hedevar was entered in the race in what was widely seen as an attempt by Whiteley to reproduce the Woodward Stakes' early speed that had allowed Damascus to win over a tired Dr. Fager. The move prompted Nerud's famous quip that "there's no one horse in the world that can beat" Dr. Fager.

The handicaps imposed on the two rivals were extraordinary. Both colts had proved able to carry weight and win a route, and in this contest, Dr. Fager would be assigned a stunning 135 pounds to Damascus' hardly insubstantial 130.

Damascus ran the early race well back in the small field and saved ground on the rail, letting jockey Tommy Lee and Hedevar wear down Dr.

Fager in a speed duel. Ycaza's move aboard Damascus came at the far turn, and the two quickly outclassed the runners behind Dr. Fager and Baeza. Ycaza remarked later, "I let Damascus settle, and when I saw Dr. Fager move, I asked him to run and he put in a tremendous burst of speed." It was again a match race between the two, but Dr. Fager was tired and Damascus slowly pulled ahead, by a head, then a neck, and by the finish line had stretched the lead to 2½ lengths. The final time of 1:59⅕ was a new record for the ten furlongs, and Damascus' winnings in the race made him racing's eighth millionaire. Ycaza, who had piloted both Dr. Fager and Damascus in wins against their chief rival, declined to identify which of his mounts was the better runner. "These were both great horses."

Retirement

Damascus and Dr. Fager would not meet again as racehorses. The latter would go on to set records as a handicap champion, while the career of the former was ended abruptly when he bowed a tendon during the fall racing season. Both champions would enjoy success in the breeding shed, Damascus at Claiborne Farm in Kentucky, and Dr. Fager at his Tartan Farms home in Florida, where they rivaled each other for distinction as leading sires and broodmare sires.

During the 1969 Triple Crown races Majestic Prince, outside, and Arts and Letters, on the rail, engaged in a heated rivalry.

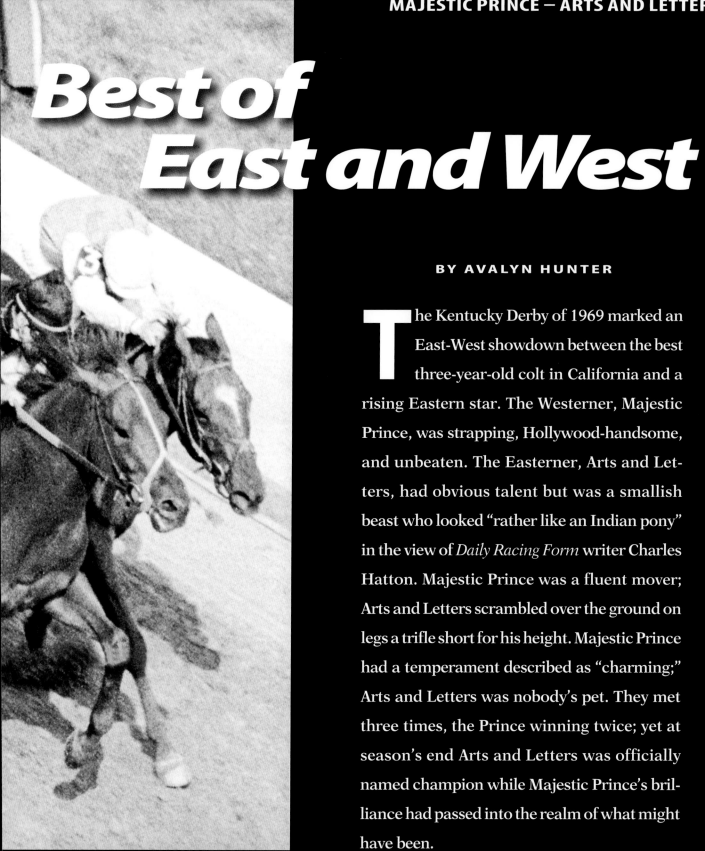

Best of East and West

BY AVALYN HUNTER

The Kentucky Derby of 1969 marked an East-West showdown between the best three-year-old colt in California and a rising Eastern star. The Westerner, Majestic Prince, was strapping, Hollywood-handsome, and unbeaten. The Easterner, Arts and Letters, had obvious talent but was a smallish beast who looked "rather like an Indian pony" in the view of *Daily Racing Form* writer Charles Hatton. Majestic Prince was a fluent mover; Arts and Letters scrambled over the ground on legs a trifle short for his height. Majestic Prince had a temperament described as "charming;" Arts and Letters was nobody's pet. They met three times, the Prince winning twice; yet at season's end Arts and Letters was officially named champion while Majestic Prince's brilliance had passed into the realm of what might have been.

Majestic Prince justified his record yearling price by going into the Kentucky Derby as the unbeaten favorite.

Majestic Prince was actually a Westerner only by courtesy, for he had been bred at Leslie Combs II's Spendthrift Farm in Kentucky. This was the home of the colt's sire, Raise a Native. A powerful chestnut with the speed of a lightning bolt and less-than-ideal forelegs, Raise a Native ran just four times before a tendon gave way. Yet he had been so impressive in that brief career, setting two Aqueduct track records and tying another, that he shared champion juvenile male honors for 1963 with Hurry to Market, winner of the prestigious Garden State Stakes. Majestic Prince was from the stallion's second crop and was produced from Gay Hostess, already the dam of the stakes-winning filly Lovely Gypsy.

Majestic Prince did not wait long to make headlines. Canadian oilman Frank McMahon purchased the handsome, well-grown colt at the 1967 Keeneland July sale for $250,000, then a world record for a yearling at auction. In the meantime, Arts and Letters took a quieter approach to life. Foaled at the Virginia farm of his breeder and owner, Paul Mellon, he was placed in due time in the care of Elliott Burch, Mellon's longtime trainer and a veteran horseman whose skills would earn him admission to the National Museum of Racing's Hall of Fame in 1980. Burch came from a distinguished family of trainers, as his father, Preston Burch, and his grandfather William Burch had preceded him into the Hall of Fame.

Neither colt covered himself with glory as a juvenile. Arts and Letters did not win until his fourth race, a seven-furlong maiden special weight at Belmont on September 25. He followed with an easy win in allowance company but was fourth in the important Pimlico-Laurel Futurity on November 2, closing his first season.

Majestic Prince did not even make his first start until after Arts and Letters had gone to winter quarters. Sent into training with Hall of Fame

jockey John Longden, who had ridden Count Fleet to victory in the 1943 Triple Crown, the colt bucked his shins, and Longden gave him plenty of time to recover and mature. The jockey-turned-trainer had an advantage on most conditioners in that he often personally exercised his charge in the mornings; he could feel for himself how Majestic Prince was progressing rather than rely on an exercise rider's reports.

Realistically, Majestic Prince's two starts at two were merely early starts on his sophomore cam-

Owner/breeder Paul Mellon and Arts and Letters

The winning connections of Majestic Prince included trainer Johnny Longden, third from right, who also had won the Derby as a jockey.

paign. He won both — a maiden special weight at Bay Meadows and an allowance at Santa Anita — before moving into stakes company. In succession the colt took four stakes races at Santa Anita, ending his skein with the Santa Anita Derby. In that race Majestic Prince was eased in the stretch and still won by eight lengths, leading racing pundits to conclude he was either the best of a weak bunch in California or a very good horse indeed. In hindsight, there was truth to both sides — only four of Majestic Prince's nine rivals in the Santa Anita Derby ever won a stakes race of any caliber, but Majestic Prince would prove himself one of the two best colts of his generation.

While Majestic Prince clearly dominated the West Coast sophomores of 1969, Arts and Letters was just one of a group of rising contenders in the East. The early leader was 1968 champion juvenile male Top Knight, who won a division of the Bahamas Stakes and the Flamingo Stakes at Hialeah and the Florida Derby at Gulfstream Park; he was also second in the Everglades Stakes, the traditional prep for the Flamingo. In three of those races, he faced Arts and Letters, who had won the Everglades by three lengths while in receipt of ten pounds (112 pounds to 122 pounds) but was a fairly beaten second at level weights in the Flamingo and the Florida Derby. In between those races, Arts and Letters sandwiched in a second-place finish to Al Hattab in the Fountain of Youth Stakes.

Arts and Letters finally punched his Derby ticket on April 24 with a resounding fifteen-length score over a relatively modest field in the Blue Grass Stakes at Keeneland, just nine days before the Kentucky Derby. Many had thought that Majestic Prince would also start in the Blue Grass, but Longden elected to put the colt in the seven-furlong Stepping Stone Purse on April 26 instead, avoiding both the improving Arts and Letters in the Blue Grass and the very fast Ack Ack in the Derby Trial on April 28. (For the record, Ack Ack set a new track record in winning the one-mile Trial.) Majestic Prince duly won his Derby prep by six easy lengths.

While some might have wondered whether Longden was ducking tough competition, in retro-

spect the choice was doubtless the right one. Longden did not want his charge knocked off form for the Derby by a hard battle in a lesser race. Further, there had always been some doubt as to the durability of Majestic Prince's underpinnings. Though a grand-looking animal, he had the suspicious ankles of his grandsire, the great Native Dancer, and sire, Raise a Native. As a precaution, Longden had fired the colt's ankles prior to the Prince's racing career, hoping to tighten the joints and make them less vulnerable to injury. The colt's easy races leading up to the Derby were everything Longden could have wished, getting the Prince into top condition without overstressing his legs.

Despite the doubts regarding the quality of his competition, Majestic Prince was the 7-5 favorite when he pranced to the post for the ninety-fifth

Majestic Prince managed to stave off Arts and Letters by a shrinking head in the Preakness.

Kentucky Derby, four-time Kentucky Derby winner Bill Hartack in the saddle as he had been throughout the colt's career. Top Knight was the second choice at 23-10; Dike, the Wood Memorial winner, was at 21-5; and Arts and Letters was the fourth choice at 22-5. The rest of the field consisted of the longshots Ocean Roar, Traffic Mark, Fleet Allied, and Rae Jet, none at less than 28-1.

Majestic Prince was the last into the starting gate but was away in midpack. Along with Arts and Letters, he stalked the early pace set by Ocean Roar and assumed by Top Knight. Then Braulio Baeza moved on Arts and Letters, sending the Rokeby Stable colt up to challenge the tiring Top Knight. By the mile marker Arts and Letters was on top by half a length, but Majestic Prince had dead aim on him and was moving powerfully.

It looked as though Majestic Prince would sweep by with the same ease with which he had conquered his earlier rivals, but Arts and Letters had other ideas. The son of the great European champion Ribot dug in as Majestic Prince surged to a half-length lead at the stretch call. Inch by painful inch, Arts and Letters cut back into the Prince's lead while Dike closed steadily on the leading pair. But there was no quit in Majestic Prince; challenged hard for the first time since the second race of his career, when he had hung on to win by a nose, he drove on gamely to win by a slowly shrinking neck over Arts and Letters. Dike was another half-length away in third.

Not only had Majestic Prince become only the third horse to win the Derby while unbeaten (the others were Regret in 1915 and Morvich in 1922), but he helped put his trainer and jockey into the record books as well. Longden became the first man to win the Derby both as a jockey and as a trainer while Hartack tied Eddie Arcaro's record of five Kentucky Derby wins. Majestic Prince was a national hero, and public admiration of the colt only

soared higher when, with Longden in the saddle, he clocked his final pre-Preakness workout of four furlongs in :45 flat. That was only one-fifth of a second off the then-existing world's record for a half-mile (according to Bob Maisel's "The Morning After" column in the *Baltimore Sun* of May 16, 1969), and Majestic Prince did it with apparent ease.

Behind the scenes, however, things were not quite as rosy as they looked. Longden was concerned with the Prince's ankles, which were showing hints of inflammation. Not much, not nearly enough to keep the colt from the Preakness, but there. In the meantime, Arts and Letters was also working sharply, turning in a final work of 1:11 — equaling the fastest six furlongs posted to that time at Pimlico's spring meeting — and the normally conservative Burch seemed not only unconcerned but even pleased.

The running of the Preakness itself had plenty of controversy. Sent off at 3-5, Majestic Prince seemed rank early. He brushed with Arts and Letters coming out of the gate, then bore out on the Rokeby Stable colt heading into the first turn. Arts and Letters, already in close quarters with Al Hattab lugging in from his outside, checked his stride, though estimates of how much ground he lost probably had much to do with where a given observer's money was riding.

Dropping 4½ lengths behind third-place Majestic Prince at the half-mile call, Arts and Letters went after the Prince as the latter assumed the lead close to the mile mark. At the stretch call Majestic Prince was a length on top, but Arts and Letters was closing. And was the Derby winner's stride growing a trifle shorter, a little less fluent? Perhaps, but there was just enough stamina, speed, and heart left to stave off Arts and Letters by a shrinking head.

The race was not over when the finish line was crossed, for Baeza wasted no time in claiming foul against Hartack and Majestic Prince. He claimed

Arts and Letters won the Belmont Stakes with authority while Majestic Prince, fatigued from his Triple Crown efforts, finished a fading second.

that the crowding on the first turn had cost Arts and Letters four or five lengths, more than enough to account for the loss, and that Majestic Prince was primarily at fault. That claim sent the stewards into prolonged consultation with Hartack, with the tapes of the race, and with one another, while the connections of the two colts and the bettors in the stands held their collective breath. Majestic Prince stood in the winner's circle, his withers draped with the traditional blanket of black-eyed Susans, but no one was at all sure whether he would get to stay there. At long last the "Official" sign blinked on; after twenty-seven agonizing minutes the foul claim had been disallowed, and Majestic Prince was finally crowned the official victor. (Fred Colwill, Pimlico's chief steward, later explained that while Arts and Letters had indeed suffered from the crowding on the first turn, Majestic Prince could not be singled out as the primary culprit.)

Controversy erupted again the next day, May 18, when Longden announced to the press that he wanted to skip the Belmont with Majestic Prince. The horse, he said, had lost nearly one hundred pounds and was tired and in need of rest. In truth, Longden suspected there was something more wrong with the colt; the uncharacteristic rankness and bearing out during the Preakness suggested discomfort. But the trainer could not quite put his finger on any problem beyond general wear and tear; there was nothing specific that he could point to and say, "Majestic Prince is injured and cannot run in the Belmont."

Pressure, both from fans and from the racing press, mounted. They wanted to see the Prince run. For McMahon, there was also the pressure of history. He knew full well that he would likely never again have a horse with a chance to win the Triple Crown. Ultimately, the decision was his to make. And on May 22, Majestic Prince shipped to Belmont Park.

Arts and Letters, meanwhile, was blooming despite the rigors of running grueling races back to back. Burch thought that the only thing his colt needed was a shot of confidence, and in an unexpected move, the trainer decided that the place for the colt to get that confidence was in the Metropolitan Handicap on May 30, a mere eight days before the Belmont. Not only did Arts and Letters win by 2½ lengths over the older Nodouble but he returned to the barn in fine fettle.

Compared to the fireworks of the preceding five weeks, the Belmont itself was a sad anticlimax, for the much-anticipated duel between Majestic Prince and Arts and Letters never materialized. Arts and Letters settled behind Dike early, took the lead at the mile marker, and drew away thereafter, winning by 5½ lengths. Majestic Prince never got closer than 1½ lengths to Arts and Letters at any stage of the race and was losing ground at the end, though he did overhaul the tiring Dike for second.

The Belmont proved to be the passing of the torch from Majestic Prince, clearly the best horse of the spring, to Arts and Letters, who did not lose again in 1969. He finished his season with dominating scores in the Jim Dandy Stakes, Travers Stakes, Woodward Stakes, and Jockey Club Gold Cup.

While Majestic Prince struggled with inflamed ankles, splints, and osselets (calcium deposits on the ankles) — a series of nagging problems that eventually saw him retired to stud in February 1970 without ever having raced again — Arts and Letters became the acknowledged champion of the division and was voted Horse of the Year for 1969. In the *Daily Racing Form/Morning Telegraph* poll for champion three-year-old male, Arts and Letters received 208 votes against 88 for Majestic Prince, seemingly a clear vote of confidence in his superiority.

Yet, there were those who still wondered what might have been had Majestic Prince remained healthy. Veteran handicapper Kenny Noe Jr. clearly was one, for at the end of the season, he made Arts and Letters and Majestic Prince co-high weights at 136 pounds atop the *Daily Racing Form*'s Free Handicap, ten pounds clear of their nearest rivals in the sophomore division and four pounds higher than champion handicapper Nodouble. He justified his decision by pointing to the Prince's brilliance in the spring, prior to the colt's injuries.

Even now, decades later, the debate over which colt was truly the better continues. Ironically, Arts and Letters, though the official champion, trailed Majestic Prince into the Hall of Fame by six years, Majestic Prince having been given the honor in 1988 while Arts and Letters was not inducted until 1994. And when *The Blood-Horse* polled a panel of racing experts and historians to rate the one hundred greatest horses of the twentieth century, Majestic Prince ranked forty-sixth while Arts and Letters was rated sixty-seventh.

So it is that the rivalry continues, not on the racetrack, but in the memories of human beings.

Affirmation

# of Greatness

Affirmed, inside, and Alydar dueled until the end in an epic Belmont Stakes.

BY RENA BAER

The New York Yankees and the Los Angeles Dodgers meeting for the tenth time in the World Series, twenty years after the Dodgers abandoned Brooklyn. Chris Evert and Martina Navratilova, their classic consistency versus power, in the finals of Wimbledon. College basketball powerhouses Kentucky and Duke having the last dance at the NCAA tournament. Could 1978 have been any better for sports rivalries? It's doubtful, particularly because it also was the year of Affirmed and Alydar.

These two magnificent Thoroughbreds raced lockstep into history in 1978, their names joined at the hip for perpetuity. Their matchup in the Belmont Stakes that year is considered one of the greatest races of all time and replays still summon goose bumps.

Both descended from one of the greatest sires of modern times, Raise a Native. Alydar claimed him as a sire; Affirmed, as a grandsire. Big things were expected of these two colts, who came into the world in 1975, Affirmed at Louis Wolfson's Harbor View Farm in Ocala, Florida, which had raced Raise a Native, and Alydar at the storied Calumet Farm in Lexington, Kentucky.

Calumet's roots traced to William Wright, who in 1888 as a thirty-seven-year-old baking powder salesman put his $3,500 savings into producing his own product, which he named Calumet. It turned out he had found the right ingredients for success. By the start of World War I, Calumet Baking Powder was in almost every kitchen in the United States.

Wright amassed a growing fortune from his business and began buying Standardbred horses. In

Lucille Parker Markey was driven trackside for Alydar's Blue Grass Stakes.

1924 he purchased four hundred acres of rolling hills in Lexington, where he could raise his trotters. The property became known as Calumet Farm.

As Wright became further involved with the farm and his horses, he started handing more control of his company to his son Warren, who took over as chairman in 1914. Much more of a corporate maven, the younger Wright was intent on expanding profits through tighter management and by stomping the competition with some less-than-scrupulous marketing campaigns. As Calumet Baking's specious

claims elicited scrutiny from the Federal Trade Commission, the elder Wright drew even further away from the business and closer to his horses.

Still, William Wright was dead set against his son's proposal to merge the company with Postum for $32 million. The younger Wright was convinced, and rightly so, that the flush days of the 1920s were soon to end.

After a weeklong standoff, William Wright gave in to his son, and in 1928 Calumet Baking became part of Postum, which would eventually become General Foods. The younger Wright stayed on as president of Calumet Baking, in name mostly, but left the company in 1931, the year his father died.

When Warren Wright's ensuing Chicago political career ended up in shambles, he headed to the Bluegrass to create a racing empire.

Bored by trotters and much more enamored by Thoroughbreds, Wright decided to make the switch. But the transition to raising and racing top-bred Thoroughbreds bore very lackluster results until Wright hired Ben Jones to take over training duties in 1939, a year after the trainer had won the Derby with Lawrin. With Jones and his son, Jimmy, at the helm, Calumet took off, starting with 1941 Triple Crown winner Whirlaway. The farm's success continued after Wright died in 1950, leaving his $20 million estate to his widow, Lucille.

Lucille Wright soon became Lucille Markey, wife of Admiral Gene Markey, a decorated World War II veteran who insisted on being addressed by his

naval rank. A Hollywood so-
cialite and screenwriter, Markey transformed his fourth,
and last, wife into somewhat
of a celebrity. (His succession
of wives included Joan Ben-
nett, Hedy Lamarr, and Myrna
Loy.) The admiral turned out
to be a devoted partner, and
over the next quarter century
the pair enjoyed their position
in high society. In fact, Lucille
Markey named Alydar as a
contraction of "Aly, Darling,"
the salutation with which she
had greeted her friend Prince
Aly Khan.

By the time Alydar came
along in1975, the Markeys

Trainer John Veitch and Alydar

were in their twilight years. Ben Jones had passed
away, and his son, who had taken the reins at Calumet from his father, had long since moved on. In
April 1976, the Markeys hired the relatively young
and reserved John Veitch, former assistant trainer
to Elliot Burch at Rokeby Stables and son of Hall of
Fame trainer Sylvester Veitch. Calumet had fallen
on some rough years, and the Markeys were looking
for a trainer who could restore the farm's glory.

Despite the new blood, Calumet's decline continued as the new trainer's barn dwindled from
twenty-four horses to nine at the end of 1976.

"I went to [the Markey's] home in Florida in December to resign at the end of that year after having
had the job for only about nine months," Veitch told
The Blood-Horse in 2007. "Mrs. Markey would not
accept my resignation and explained to me that she
had given me a lot of bad horses to train and I would
have better material to work with and that is how it
turned out."

Alydar, a handsome chestnut, showed much
promise. Veitch realized from his early training
days that the Raise a Native colt was a quick
learner.

Raise a Native had been injured and retired to
stud after only four starts, yet his brilliance earned
him a share in the 1963 two-year-old championship
along with Hurry to Market. Alydar's dam, Sweet
Tooth, was not so stellar, but she was stakes-placed
at two and a good allowance winner at three and
four. She was from Calumet's Blue Delight family,
which had produced 1952 champion three-year-old
filly Real Delight, Kentucky Oaks winners Bubbley
(1953) and Princess Turia (1956), as well as 1968
Kentucky Derby and Preakness winner Forward
Pass.

By the time Alydar began training seriously early
in his two-year-old season, Veitch had even more
reason to be optimistic. The colt's older half sister
Our Mims was improving as she matured, having

placed in the Demoiselle and Tempted stakes at two. And Alydar himself was showing signs of being more precocious than Our Mims. By June 1977, he was ready to race.

Affirmed's sire was Exclusive Native, who, like his sire Raise a Native, was a superb runner whose racing career was cut short by injuries. Affirmed's dam, Won't Tell You, came from a solid family of hard knockers. Though Affirmed came from good bloodlines, he wasn't quite "born into" the same regal scenario as Alydar.

Louis and Patrice Wolfson, owners of Affirmed

Although Exclusive Native and Affirmed were products of Harbor View Farm, owner Louis Wolfson's roots didn't run as deep as those of Calumet and the Wrights. The son of Lithuanian immigrants, Wolfson, born in 1912, and his seven siblings grew up in Jacksonville, where their father was a scrap-metal dealer. As a teenager Wolfson boxed professionally under the name "Kid Wolf," earning $25 to $100 a fight.

An outstanding athlete, Wolfson went on to play football at the University of Georgia, reportedly demanding, and receiving, $100 a month to play. He left college after two years, raised $10,000 from his family and a wealthy Georgia football fan, and started Florida Pipe and Supply Company. By age twenty-eight he was a millionaire, expanding his construction firm into shipbuilding, chemicals, and money lending. Wolfson became nationally know in 1955 when he unsuccessfully attempted a hostile takeover of retailer Montgomery Ward.

He later ran into legal troubles stemming from stock sales and spent a year in a prison in the late 1960s, which led to his crusade for prison reform. In 1971 Wolfson became headlines again when he filed a complaint against then Miami radio host Larry King, now of CNN fame, for allegedly pocketing $5,000 of a $25,000 payment to New Orleans District Attorney Jim Garrison, who was investigating John F. Kennedy's assassination. King was arrested and charged with grand larceny, but the charges were dismissed because the statute of limitations had run out. Still, King was fired after Wolfson wrote his employer complaining "King was a menace to the public" and the station should pay for King's "treatment in a mental institution for six months ..."

Meanwhile, Wolfson had established Harbor View Farm near Ocala, Florida, in 1960, and his success on that front had started with his purchase of Raise a Native in 1962. Affirmed came along thirteen years later, under the tutelage of Laz Barrera, who had trained Bold Forbes to Kentucky Derby and Belmont Stakes wins in 1976 for another stable.

Barrera had always been a top trainer. The Havana native, one of twelve children, had obtained his license at Oriental Park in the early 1940s before moving to Mexico City in 1945. He became Mexico's leading trainer but gave all that up to take one horse, a $6,000 claimer named Destructo, to Hollywood Park. When that horse was claimed from him, he landed at Alfred G. Vanderbilt's stable and then at the stable of New York restauranteur Emile Dolce. Barrera quickly showed his training prowess and business took off. When Ivan Parke retired in the late 1970s, Wolfson chose Barrera as his replacement.

Barrera was quite a character and known for his colorful quotes, in addition to his skills as a trainer. He immediately recognized in Affirmed's juvenile year that the chestnut colt was much more than raw speed.

Affirmed, at 14-1, won his first race, a 5½-furlong maiden special, by 4½ lengths May 24, 1977, at Belmont, while being ridden by an apprentice jockey, Bernie Gonzalez, who was as green as his mount.

"Any colt who can win his first race has accomplished something; when he can win it like Affirmed did, he is something special," wrote race writer Joe Hirsch in the *Daily Racing Form*.

Word already had gotten out that Alydar also was something special. The colt's exceptional morning workouts had trainers seemingly dodging him in the entries, causing fields not to fill and leaving Veitch no choice but to make his first start a stakes race.

It was in the Youthful Stakes on June 15 that Alydar and Affirmed first crossed paths, but the meeting certainly did not portend the future rivalry. The unraced Alydar, at 9-5 with Eddie Maple aboard, was made the favorite, followed by Affirmed, ridden by Angel Cordero Jr. But the odds were as close as the two horses would get. Affirmed stalked the leader, Buck Mountain, pulling away at midstretch to win the 5½-furlong race. Alydar, whose exit from the gate lacked urgency, got trapped in the early going, and though able to stage a nice late rally, he finished fifth in the eleven-horse field.

Nine days later Alydar got it figured out in a 5½-furlong maiden special weight. A regular rider for Veitch, Maple was in the saddle again, guiding the favored Alydar to an almost seven-length win in a zippy 1:04⅕.

Horseplayers liked what they saw, and when Alydar and Affirmed reached the gate for the Great American on July 6, in what would become the real beginning of their legendary rivalry, Alydar, ridden by Maple, had been bet down to 4-5. Affirmed, Cordero in the saddle, was third choice at 4.6-1 behind Going Investor.

The interloper was quickly cut out of the picture as it became a two-horse contest. Affirmed raced to the lead, with Alydar waiting outside, 2½ lengths back in fourth, to make his move. Heading into the stretch, Alydar, with a five-pound weight break (117-122), surged ahead of Affirmed with a powerful run and won the 5½-furlong race by 3½ lengths in 1:03⅗, three-fifths of a second off the track record. Alydar had handed Affirmed his first defeat.

The two colts parted ways, with Affirmed heading west to take the Hollywood Juvenile Championship with Laffit Pincay in the irons, and Alydar remaining in the Northeast to win the Tremont and Sapling stakes under Maple.

Barrera brought Affirmed back east to Saratoga for the Hopeful Stakes on August 27, with a prep in the Sanford Stakes ten days earlier.

Pincay did not want to travel all the way to New York to ride Affirmed at Saratoga. Angel Cordero, who had twice ridden Affirmed, opted instead to

Alydar winning the Champagne Stakes

ride Darby Creek Road, who he thought could handle more distance and would be the better horse for the longer run, both literally and figuratively. In their stead, Barrera chose the young Steve Cauthen, who had burst onto the racing scene in 1976 as a sixteen-year-old, winning 240 races.

"The Kid," sporting Harbor View's familiar pink-and-black silks, rode Affirmed to a 2¾-length win in the Sanford, earning a spot on the colt for the Hopeful, Saratoga's most prestigious two-year-old race.

The Hopeful drew a talented, albeit small, field that included Alydar and Darby Creek Road. Despite the high-end lineup, the race turned into a match between Affirmed and Alydar in the stretch. Though Tilt Up challenged briefly at the head of the stretch, the big two drove away from him, Affirmed on the inside, Maple driving Alydar hard on the outside. Affirmed, holding a straight and true course, edged ahead to win the 6½-furlong race by a half-length in a stakes record 1:15⅖, leaving Cordero to

finish last on Darby Creek Road and probably to wonder what he had given up.

The rivals' next meeting, in Belmont's seven-furlong Futurity, was an even closer fight, with Affirmed nosing out Alydar at the wire.

With a score to settle in the upcoming Champagne, Veitch thought a change in jockeys might help and decided to replace Maple with Jorge Velasquez, whose aggressiveness he thought would be more suited to Alydar's one-strong-run style.

Stretched to a mile in the Champagne, Alydar had enough track to make his one strong run past Affirmed for a 1¼-length victory. Lest anyone presume that Alydar had the upper hand at longer distances, Affirmed turned the tables two weeks later in the 1¹⁄₁₆-mile Laurel Futurity, a heart-pounding race in which he edged Alydar by a neck.

The public, meanwhile, was very much divided into two camps. Though Affirmed led the rivalry, winning four of their six meetings as two-year-olds and taking the juvenile championship, Alydar supporters remained convinced their horse was on the cusp of greatness, a stride away from reversing the trend.

Racing fans would have to wait until the world's most famous race, the Kentucky Derby, to find out. Affirmed headed to California for the winter, and Alydar shipped to Florida but not before running second to Believe It in the Remsen. After a couple months off from racing, Alydar and Velasquez came back to win an allowance race, the Flamingo Stakes, and the Florida Derby by two lengths over Believe It.

Meanwhile, out in California the skies opened, closing only intermittently and dampening Affirmed's training and Barrera's spirits.

Before the San Felipe on March 18, 1978, Barrera had his doubts that Affirmed, with all the missed training from the rain, was up to the task, but the trainer was philosophical.

"The San Felipe is just a small stroll in the sunshine," he told *Sports Illustrated*. "I'm looking down the road toward the Kentucky Derby. That is what matters.

"We are going to have to fight Alydar like we did last year. My horse, he will not meet Alydar before the Derby. But that day we put on the heavy gloves. It will be him and us. Today we just lace the gloves up and spar."

All it took Affirmed was one good, well-timed jab to win the 1 1/16-mile race. The colt raced off the lead until he was ready to pounce, Cauthen springing him to a two-length lead at the wire. The young jockey, anxious to keep riding Affirmed, had followed Barrera to California despite all the opportunities he was missing on the East Coast.

His loyalty was rewarded. When Cauthen was handed a five-day suspension for making no effort to keep his mount straight just after the start of a minor stakes race, the Wolfsons made it clear the "The Kid" would not lose his mount. During the suspension Pincay rode Affirmed to an eight-length win in the Santa Anita Derby on April 2, but Cauthen was back in the saddle two weeks later to take the Hollywood Derby by two lengths.

Though Affirmed was four for four as a three-year-old, popular sentiment still tilted toward Alydar. The Calumet colt had returned to his old Kentucky home to run in the Blue Grass Stakes, a sentimental and sensational race, despite the absence of Affirmed.

Keeneland president Ted Bassett had the Markeys, both confined to wheelchairs, driven to the far rail to watch the April 27 race. During the post parade, Velasquez and Alydar slipped away for a quick visit with the couple. "Here's your baby, my lady," the jockey told Lucille Markey.

On cue, Alydar gave the Markeys an unforgettable curtain call, blowing by the leaders on the final turn to win the 1 1/8-mile race by an impressive thirteen lengths. The crowd went wild, though some wondered with the Kentucky Derby only nine days away whether Velasquez should have eased up Alydar at the end.

Barrera, meanwhile, had shipped Affirmed to Kentucky for the Derby. He wanted people to see his horse work and quell the buzz that Affirmed wasn't as good as his record might indicate.

"All I hear in Kentucky is that Affirmed cannot win the Derby because he was bred in Florida and raced in California this winter," he told *Sports Illustrated*. "Florida and California are part of the United States, aren't they? Affirmed has not been winning his races in China."

All the Derby hype centered on Affirmed and Alydar and the rivalry that had developed between them as two-year-olds. But the other nine horses in the field could not be overlooked. All the winners of the major prep races had managed to get to Kentucky uninjured. But that didn't stop Alydar from going off as the favorite at 6-5 and Affirmed as second choice at 9-5.

"This is no pickin' chicken party," Barrera said before the race.

More than 131,000 racing fans gathered at Churchill Downs on Derby Day to watch two of racing's greatest horses match strides on the fast track, knowing they were going to see something exceptional.

Alydar, again leisurely out of the starting gate, didn't seem to be able to get hold of the track, winding up seventeen lengths behind the leaders. Affirmed sat in third place before bolting to a two-length lead at the top of the stretch. Meanwhile, Alydar had begun a very late charge, running outside down the stretch. Affirmed held stubbornly to his lead, and Alydar, though he closed the distance, finished 1½ lengths behind his rival.

Veitch was disappointed but not ready to concede

anything but the Derby to Affirmed.

"Affirmed was the best horse in the Derby," he said. "Whether he will be in the Preakness and the Belmont nobody knows. We'll have to wait and see. But Alydar will try Affirmed again in both races."

Veitch told reporters before the Preakness that three hundred fans had written the stable right after the Derby, each advocating a different technique for beating Affirmed in the Preakness, including changing jockeys.

"One fellow wrote that we ought to send Velasquez back to Panama and keep the canal," Veitch told reporters.

Veitch stuck with his rider, but for the first time the bettors swung the pendulum in favor of Affirmed over Alydar in the Preakness. The Harbor View colt drew odds of 1-2 while the darling of Calumet went off at 9-5. Believe It sat third in line at 6-1, with Maple in the saddle. While nobody was going to make a killing at the windows, fans would witness one fine horse race.

Despite Alydar's late charge, Affirmed won the Derby by daylight.

Affirmed won the Preakness Stakes with Alydar breathing down his neck.

Affirmed led at a moderate pace from the first turn with Alydar never more than six lengths behind him. Going into the final turn, both Alydar and Believe It made their moves. Cauthen, meanwhile, was waiting to see the red-and-blue silks of Calumet before he asked his horse for his run. In the stretch Alydar appeared, and the battle was on. Alydar cut the margin to a length, to a half, to a neck, and finally to a head as the battle intensified. But Affirmed would not let Alydar go by. At the wire, the Harbor View colt led by a neck in a time of 1:54⅖, only two-fifths of a second off the race record.

As good of a race as the Preakness was, the Belmont was an all-time classic.

Alydar fans were hopeful that the longer distance of the Belmont would better suit the Calumet colt and be more of a detriment to Affirmed.

Veitch also felt beforehand that the Belmont was their best opportunity to beat Affirmed in the Triple Crown races. The thought was that both the 1½-mile distance and the surface would be more suited to Alydar. Veitch said both Churchill and Pimlico had made their track surfaces especially fast, and Belmont had never done that.

"I thought we'd have a truer test there," he said.

Barerra scoffed at the idea that a longer race would trouble Affirmed.

"Anyone who thinks he can't run the distance is crazy," he said. "This horse can run five miles; he is no stopper."

Affirmed's Preakness victory had made him the youngest horse at the time to earn a million dollars. It also put a Triple Crown victory in his sight, or at least in those of his trainer and owner. Barrera worried constantly that something would happen to his colt before the big race.

The night before the Belmont, a TV cameraman sat on top of Barrera's office, shooting the horse sleeping and getting up for his feedings. Barrera had told the two night watchmen that at the first sign Affirmed was being disturbed to call him so he could come over and tell the cameraman he had to leave.

"But there was no problem," the trainer said. "The horse slept perfect. Only I didn't."

Between the Preakness and Belmont, Veitch had spent just about every minute of every day thinking about a strategy to beat Affirmed. He had already

Affirmed and Alydar ran lockstep in an unforgettable Belmont.

decided to take off the blinkers. "But I never did decide what instructions to give the rider until we were in the paddock," he said.

He told Velasquez to stay closer to Affirmed and to take the fight to him earlier. The jockey did as he was told. In the last mile, Alydar clung to Affirmed racing in lockstep part of the way. In the home-stretch, they battled, Alydar pushing his nose in front. But Affirmed would not allow himself to get beat. With every sinew of his being he fought back, and the two horses swished under the wire. Despite the photo finish, Cauthen immediately stood up in the saddle and pumped his whip in triumph, knowing he had won the coveted Triple Crown.

Alydar also had made history by being the only horse ever to finish second in all three legs of the Triple Crown, not to mention to the same horse, Affirmed. In fact, with the exception of their first meeting, the pair finished one-two in every race they faced each other.

They met only once more, in the Travers Stakes at Saratoga, in an unsatisfying ending to a great rivalry. Affirmed, ridden by Pincay, cut off Alydar on the far turn, and though Affirmed went on to win by a wide margin, his number came down, and the victory was awarded to Alydar. The final tally was seven wins for Affirmed, five of which had come by a half-length or less, and three for Alydar.

But no matter what the score, one could not have made as much history without the other.

Belmont Stakes
Purse: $150,000 Added

8th Race Belmont Park - June 10, 1978
Purse $150,000 added. Three-year-olds. 1 1-2 Miles. Main Track. Track: Fast.
Value of race $184,300. Value to winner $110,580; second, $40,546; third, $22,116; fourth, $11,058.
Mutuel pool $1,186,662. OTB pool $1,389,646.

P#	Horse	A	Wgt	Med	Eqp	Odds	PP	1/4	1/2	1m	1¼	Str	Fin	Jockey
3	Affirmed	3	126			.60	3	1^1	1^1	1$^{1/2}$	1^{hd}	1^{hd}	1^{hd}	S Cauthen
2	Alydar	3	126			1.10	2	3$^{1/2}$	2^1	2^5	2^8	2^{12}	2^{13}	J Velasquez
1	Darby Creek Road	3	126			9.90	1	5	5	5	3$^{1/2}$	3^4	3$^{7/2}$	A Cordero Jr
4	Judge Advocate	3	126			30.10	4	2$^{1/2}$	3$^{2/2}$	4^3	5	4^{hd}	4$^{1/2}$	J Fell
5	Noon Time Spender	3	126		b	38.40	5	4^1	4^3	3$^{1/2}$	4^{hd}	5	5	R Hernandez

Off Time: 5:43 Eastern Daylight Time **Time Of Race:** :25 :50 1:14 1:37⅖ 2:01⅖ 2:26⅖
Start: Good For All **Track:** Fast.
Equipment: b for blinkers

Mutuel Payoffs
3 **Affirmed**	$3.20	$2.10	.....
2 **Alydar**		2.20	.....
1 **Darby Creek Road**			.....
No Show Mutuels Sold.			

Winner: Affirmed, ch. c. by Exclusive Native—Won't Tell You, by Crafty Admiral (Trained by L. S. Barrera).
Bred by Harbor View Farm in Fl.

Start good. Won driving.
AFFIRMED went right to the front and was rated along on the lead while remaining well out from the rail. He responded readily when challenged by ALYDAR soon after entering the backstretch, held a narrow advantage into the stretch while continuing to save ground and was under left-handed urging to prevail in a determined effort. ALYDAR, away in good order, saved ground to the first turn. He came out to go after AFFIRMED with seven furlongs remaining, raced with that rival to the stretch, reached almost even terms with AFFIRMED near the three-sixteenths pole but wasn't good enough in a stiff drive. DARBY CREEK ROAD, unhurried while being outrun early, moved around horses while rallying on the far turn but lacked a further response. JUDGE ADVOCATE broke through before the start and was finished at the far turn. NOON TIME SPENDER raced within striking distance for a mile and gave way.

Owners: (3) Harbor View Farm; (2) Calumet Farm; (1) J W Phillips; (4) O Phipps; (5) Miami Lakes Ranch
Trainers: (3) L S Barrera; (2) John M Veitch; (1) Thomas L Rondinello; (4) John W. Russell; (5) Antonio Arcodia
©EQUIBASE

BY TRACY GANTZ

P ractical people will say that Thoroughbred racehorses don't know or care whom they're running against. They simply go out on the track and do their job. Try telling that to Jack Van Berg, trainer of Alysheba. Bet Twice, who thwarted Alysheba's bid for the 1987 Triple Crown, met Alysheba on nine occasions, so often that Van Berg swears they recognized each other.

Alysheba's Stumbling Block

Alysheba's narrow victory over Bet Twice in the 1988 Iselin Handicap at Monmouth Park typified their rivalry.

"When we shipped in [to Maryland] when Alysheba was a four-year-old for the Pimlico Special, those two horses would nicker like hell every time they walked by the other's stall," Van Berg said. "They knew — those two horses knew each other."

They had every chance. Alysheba and Bet Twice faced each other over the course of three seasons at seven racetracks, from New York to California. One or the other finished first in seven of their nine meetings.

But it was their Triple Crown encounters that will always stand out. Like a thorn under Alysheba's saddle, Bet Twice threatened Alysheba in the Kentucky Derby and Preakness. In the case of the Derby, Bet Twice swerved out in the stretch and Alysheba ran up on his heels and stumbled, yet Alysheba won in one of the most miraculous recoveries in Derby history.

Alysheba stood on the brink of legend in the Belmont, one race away from immortality as the sport's twelfth Triple Crown winner. But he finished fourth while Bet Twice galloped to a 14½-length laugher.

Which horse was better? Alysheba outfinished Bet Twice five to four, captured the more historic races, and earned the year-end championships. Yet on two occasions when Bet Twice visited the winner's circle, Alysheba ran a poor fourth, and Bet Twice's Belmont victory was among the most decisive in the annals of that classic race.

Alysheba and Bet Twice both hailed from some of the finest operations in Central Kentucky. Preston Madden bred Alysheba while W.S. Farish and E.J. Hudson bred Bet Twice.

Alysheba's bloodlines and stunning looks gave him more cachet at the 1985 yearling sales. The Triple Crown flowed throughout his pedigree. His sire, Alydar, might have won the prestigious series in 1978 if not for Affirmed, and the grandsire of his dam, Bel Sheba, was none other than 1937 Triple Crown winner War Admiral.

Bet Twice didn't have as illustrious a pedigree, though his ancestors had had their share of championships. Sire Sportin' Life won some useful East Coast stakes and was a son of English Triple Crown winner Nijinsky II. Bet Twice's dam, Golden Dust, had already produced a California champion in Bold and Gold and would later foal Santa Anita

Oaks winner Golden Treat.

The disparity in their lineage emerged at the sales. Bet Twice sold for $50,000 at the 1985 Keeneland fall sale a few months after Alysheba sold for ten times that, $500,000, at the prestigious Keeneland summer sale. East Coast racetrack executive Robert P. Levy bought Bet Twice for himself; his wife, Cis-

sie; and his mother, Blanche. Texas Quarter Horse owner Clarence Scharbauer bid on Alysheba for his wife, Dorothy, and their daughter, Pam.

Two crusty horsemen with more experience than any dozen of their peers oversaw Alysheba's and Bet Twice's racing careers. Van Berg, cowboy-raised in the Midwest, loved to spin a yarn. Bet Twice's trainer, Warren A. (Jimmy) Croll, parted with as few words as possible to get his point across. Both had learned horsemanship from the ground up and knew the secrets to discovering a horse's potential.

Croll based his stable at Monmouth Park in New Jersey while Van Berg, who for years ran a nation-wide stable with divisions all over the country, was by the mid-1980s ensconced in Southern California. Thus, even though Alysheba and Bet Twice ventured as far from home as Kentucky and Illinois as two-year-olds, they didn't meet until the 1986 Breeders' Cup Juvenile, held at Santa Anita.

To that point, Bet Twice had proved himself the stronger, with victories on his home ground at Monmouth in the Sapling and in Maryland's Laurel Futurity. Alysheba had a lone victory in five starts, which is why fans dismissed him at 33-1 in the Juvenile.

Capote clinched the year-end two-year-old male championship with his front-running victory in the Juvenile. Alysheba under Bill Shoemaker and Bet Twice under Craig Perret finished third and fourth, respectively.

"They wanted Shoemaker on him," Van Berg said of the only time the legendary Hall of Fame jockey ever rode Alysheba. "Shoe rode Mrs. Scharbauer's father's horse [Tomy Lee, winner of the 1959 Kentucky Derby]."

Van Berg blamed himself for Alysheba's loss. "I didn't tell Shoe to slap him away from the gate,"

Despite nearly falling in the stretch during the Kentucky Derby, Alysheba righted himself to come home first under the Twin Spires.

In the 1987 Preakness Stakes, Alysheba defeated Bet Twice by half a length.

the trainer said.

Shoemaker found what he considered a better 1987 Kentucky Derby mount in Temperate Sil, who had defeated Alysheba and Pat Day in the Hollywood Futurity but would miss the Triple Crown because of illness. Day stuck with Alysheba for two losses at Santa Anita in early 1987 before opting for Demons Begone. Chris McCarron, returning from an injury, inherited the mount on Alysheba, one he held onto for the rest of the colt's career.

Meanwhile, on the opposite coast, in Florida, Perret was firmly established as Bet Twice's regular jockey and would ride the colt in twenty-five of his twenty-six starts. Yet, he and Bet Twice could

only win one of three Derby preps. They captured the Fountain of Youth before running fifth behind Cryptoclearance in the Florida Derby, Bet Twice's final Derby prep.

Alysheba improved enough to finish first in the Blue Grass Stakes at Keeneland, though he was disqualified for interference and placed third. What many didn't know was that Van Berg had reluctantly given the OK for veterinarian Scott Merrell to perform a standing surgery for an entrapped epiglottis on Alysheba. The colt could finally breathe properly, and Van Berg noticed a difference in Alysheba's first work following the surgery.

With those spotty Derby preps on Alysheba's and

Bet Twice owned the 1987 Belmont, with Alysheba finishing fourth.

Bet Twice's records, few expected the colts to launch an epic rivalry in the 1987 Kentucky Derby. Arkansas Derby victor Demons Begone went off as the 2-1 favorite while Alysheba was sixth choice at 8-1 and Bet Twice next at 10-1.

"I thought Demons Begone was the horse to beat," Robert Levy said. "But I thought we had enough speed to stalk and be in position. I've always thought that if you're in front at the top of the stretch, you've got a good chance of winning the Derby."

That's exactly where Perret had Bet Twice when the field swung out of the final turn. The jockey had avoided the traffic jam on the first turn as well as Demons Begone, who bled badly and was pulled up on the backstretch.

Alysheba had trouble from the start. "I was getting slammed," McCarron said of the run to the first turn. "I finally had to snatch up and that put me much farther back than I wanted to be in a large field like that."

It also gave McCarron a good view of quite a bit of crowding ahead of him.

"It was a very rough-run first turn," he said, "and I was just back there praying that nobody falls."

McCarron shifted Alysheba to the outside on the backstretch, avoiding the potential pileup and keeping dirt from flying in the colt's face. They moved up rapidly to take aim at Bet Twice in the stretch. Then the two horses nearly collided.

"Everyone says we came out on Alysheba," Levy

In Monmouth Park's 1987 Haskell Invitational Handicap, Bet Twice once again got the measure of a fast-closing Alysheba.

As four-year-olds, Bet Twice, inside, drew first blood in the rivalry by winning the 1988 Pimlico Special over Lost Code and Cryptoclearance with Alysheba, second from left, finishing fourth.

said. "But I think he ran up on our heels. Would we have come down? I don't know. But that got us beat more than anything else. We were pretty cut up behind."

Alysheba nearly went to his knees with a wall of horses on his heels. Somehow, he managed to right himself, stay in the race, and pass Bet Twice to win by three-quarters of a length.

"Bet Twice ducked out under Craig Perret's left hand," McCarron said, "and we clipped heels and stumbled badly. Showing the incredible athlete that Alysheba was, he picked himself back up and went on."

Alysheba and Bet Twice may have emerged from their battle a little stiff and sore. However, two weeks later they were ready again, this time in Maryland for the Preakness. Though he had finished second in the Derby, Bet Twice wasn't receiving accolades as Alysheba's closest rival — yet. Alysheba, as befitted a Derby victor, went off as the 2-1 favorite, with Bet Twice the 5-1 fourth choice behind Cryptoclearance and Gulch.

In the days leading up to the race, Van Berg was irked because an exercise rider had worked Alysheba slower than the trainer had wanted.

"Jimmy Croll told Craig Perret, 'Craig, you will

not have to worry about Alysheba because he acts dead around that barn,' " Van Berg said.

When Alysheba stepped onto the Pimlico track for the race, the fans cheered and clapped so loudly that he kicked his heels into the air. Perret turned to Croll and remarked, "If you think that horse is dead, you'd better take another look at him."

Perret didn't give Bet Twice a chance to take another look. He kept his colt ahead of Alysheba in third, staying off the rail.

"I was able to get to the part of the track I wanted early," the jockey said, "and if anybody wanted the rail, they were welcomed to it. I didn't want any part of it."

McCarron saw that Perret was riding very confidently, but he also knew Alysheba had plenty of gas in his tank. Accordingly, he didn't ask the colt to make his move until the last sixteenth of a mile.

Alysheba handed Bet Twice a half-length defeat to garner the second leg of the Triple Crown. Critics said Perret had moved too soon and called for his replacement, but Levy denied that his rider acted prematurely.

"Alysheba won fair and square," Levy said, "and again we had the lead at the top of the stretch."

After the race Perret noted how evenly matched the two horses were. "I have confidence in Bet Twice," the jockey said. "Alysheba might be a half-length better, but if he ever makes a mistake, I'll be there."

Perret felt more confident three weeks later going into the 1½-mile Belmont Stakes because Bet Twice was responding well to Croll's regimen to get him ready for the marathon distance.

On May 31 Croll sent Bet Twice seven furlongs in 1:26 after first having Perret gallop him a mile. "I did not let him pull up and catch his breath before the work," Croll said. "He galloped a mile, worked five-eighths of a mile, then spurted a quarter-mile."

Perret told Levy that they were unbeatable.

"That's what I thought in the Preakness," Levy replied. "But I was confident."

What Levy wasn't confident of was winning a million-dollar bonus attached to the Triple Crown races. The horse with the most points in the three races would earn the bonus. Alysheba was leading in points, and the only way Bet Twice could grab the money was if he could win and Alysheba finished fourth or worse. Levy saw no chance of that happening.

Croll didn't ship to Belmont Park in New York until the morning of the race. "We were at Monmouth," Levy said, "and Jimmy felt that the horse was better off sleeping in his own stall."

Whether it was the good night's sleep or simply Bet Twice's moment, Levy's colt turned in the most dominating performance of his career. Before the nine horses had traveled a mile, Perret had Bet Twice in front en route to a 14½-length trouncing of Cryptoclearance, who had finished fourth in the Derby and third in the Preakness. And Alysheba indeed finished fourth, allowing Bet Twice to pick up the bonus as well.

"I didn't wager on Bet Twice because I seldom bet on stakes," Croll said after the race. "But I thought he was an overlay at 8-1."

Scharbauer, bitterly disappointed at being denied a Triple Crown, had the class to step up and congratulate Levy in the winner's circle.

Instead of going their separate ways after the Triple Crown, Alysheba and Bet Twice met again two months later when Monmouth's management boosted the purse of the Haskell Invitational Handicap to $500,000 to draw the pair. This was Bet Twice's home turf, and he, Alysheba, and Lost Code, who had bypassed the Triple Crown events, put on quite a show for the fans.

Lost Code winged to the front and stubbornly

kept going, even when the Triple Crown duo came after him. The gallant Lost Code finished third by two necks to Bet Twice and Alysheba.

Levy credited Perret with the victory. "Craig put Chris against the rail and wouldn't let him out," Levy said. "Alysheba was flying, but we had the momentum."

Even McCarron admits that he didn't ride as smartly as he could have. "I'll take the heat for the Haskell," he said. "I screwed up the Haskell."

The pair met one more time in 1987, but the sloppy track at Saratoga for the Travers Stakes didn't help either of them. Mud-loving Java Gold won while Bet Twice finished fifth, more than thirteen lengths behind the winner and eight lengths ahead of Alysheba in sixth.

Bet Twice ended his year unplaced in the Woodward Stakes at Belmont. Alysheba won the Super Derby and lost the Breeders' Cup Classic by only a nose to older Kentucky Derby hero Ferdinand. That cemented Ferdinand as Horse of the Year and gave Alysheba the champion three-year-old male title.

Bet Twice wasn't through with Alysheba, however. The pair would meet three more times as four-year-olds in 1988. Despite the fact that Bet Twice's knees and front ankles required some repair work between seasons and the soreness would eventually get the better of him, he let Alysheba know that victories would never come easily.

As Alysheba dominated California that winter, Bet Twice became forgotten with only a couple of outings at Keeneland that spring to remind anyone of his former glory.

When the May 14 Pimlico Special approached, track officials offered an extra $100,000, boosting the purse to $600,000, if the winner had been nominated to the Triple Crown. They were trying to lure Alysheba as well as Lost Code and Cryptoclearance,

At the Meadowlands in 1988, Alysheba continued his dominance, winning the Meadowlands Cup over Slew City Slew with Bet Twice fourth.

Alysheba closed his career with a thrilling victory in the 1988 Breeders' Cup Classic.

but they also snared Bet Twice.

The Triple Crown quartet completely outclassed older horses Little Bold John and Lac Ouimet. But it was 6-1 fourth-choice Bet Twice who overhauled Lost Code to win by three-quarters of a length. Alysheba finished fourth behind Cryptoclearance as the 3-5 favorite.

Van Berg blamed himself for not have prepared Alysheba adequately for the task. "I didn't have a fit horse," he said. "I learned a lesson today. I should have come here with him a month early to give him a chance to train over the deeper racetrack."

Now fans began viewing Bet Twice as a true rival for Alysheba and wanted Alysheba to get another chance at him. A cash inducement, doubling a $250,000 purse to $500,000, attracted the pair to the August 27 Philip H. Iselin Handicap at Monmouth. A fit Alysheba collared front-runner Slew City Slew and Bet Twice to beat his old nemesis by three-quarters of a length, Gulch getting third.

"He fired just like I wanted, but not enough," Perret said of Bet Twice. "Alysheba was just a little bit better today." Or as Van Berg told Croll, "It was my turn, Jimmy."

Alysheba and Bet Twice squared off one final time, in the October 14 Meadowlands Cup, the purse for which was raised from $500,000 to $600,000. By then, however, Bet Twice was past his prime. Alysheba defeated Slew City Slew by a neck, and Bet Twice finished fourth, seven lengths behind his rival.

"Our horse got sore and Alysheba improved," Levy said. "Alysheba was a survivor."

Alysheba ended his career with a spectacular victory in the Breeders' Cup Classic in near darkness at Churchill Downs, the crowning achievement in his 1988 Horse of the Year season. Bet Twice may not have had a championship trophy to call his own, but the $50,000 yearling proved himself a more-than-able challenger to his $500,000 rival.

CHAPTER 16

PERSONAL ENSIGN — WINNING COLORS

Personal Ensign kept her unblemished record with a gritty victory over
Kentucky Derby winner Winning Colors in the 1988 Breeders' Cup Distaff.

Color Her Perfect

BY MICHELE MACDONALD

Within less than a year between the spring of 1984 and the end of winter in 1985, two fillies were born in Kentucky that would leave imprints of their hooves and hearts on racing for at least as long as the memories of anyone who saw them run.

Yet they could not have been more different, both in the way they competed and in the teams they represented on the racetrack.

A willowy bay standing a regal 16.2 hands, Personal Ensign carried the staunch tradition of the Phipps family dynasty on her back as well as the stable's famed black silks and cherry cap while racing for breeder Ogden Phipps. Foaled on April 27, 1984, at Claiborne Farm in Paris, Kentucky, where Phipps sequestered his prized broodmare band, the daughter of Private Account often left the starting gate nonchalantly but could rush down the stretch with the fury of a tiger attacking prey. Yet, her trainer, Claude R. "Shug" McGaughey III, could not watch most of her races without a cold grip of fear on his shoulders, knowing that she went to the post with five screws in her left hind leg after a fracture that would have ended most horses' careers.

At 16.3 hands, Winning Colors bulged with the muscles of a National Football League fullback, despite her gender. Bred by Echo Valley Horse

Winning Colors held off Forty Niner in the 1988 Kentucky Derby after leading at every call.

Farm and foaled on March 14, 1985, she was plucked out of the 1986 Keeneland July select yearling sale by former Quarter Horse trainer D. Wayne Lukas for $575,000. The strapping daughter of Caro bore the gold-and-blue silks marked by a lightning bolt of flamboyant owner Eugene V. Klein, who spent $39 million over six years amassing horseflesh that could win him titles. She had one gear — full-throttle speed — and she typically required handlers on both sides to keep her volcanic energy contained while she was walking from the barn to the paddock for saddling.

The roads the two fillies traveled crossed only twice, but each encounter produced a remarkable finish. One of these races, the 1988 Breeders' Cup Distaff, would become the hallmark of the entire Breeders' Cup championship series, billed in many quarters as the greatest race of the modern era.

Marked by a distinctive white snip on her black nose, Personal Ensign arrived in McGaughey's barn at Keeneland Race Course as a two-year-old with no particular advanced billing. The trainer was just months into his new job as private conditioner for the Phipps family and was not overly impressed as he watched her work four furlongs in :50.

When the stable shipped to Saratoga, however, and she began reeling off more spirited breezes even on the deep Oklahoma training track, he began to feel a tingle of excitement. On September 28, 1986, after she circled a field of six rivals following a slow start to win a seven-furlong maiden race over a muddy Belmont Park track by 12¾ lengths in 1:22⅘, McGaughey conceded, "We were a little bit in awe. We didn't know she was that good."

About two weeks later Personal Ensign validated her talent, capturing the grade I Frizette Stakes by a head over the more battle-tested filly, Collins. It appeared then that anything was possible for her. But no one could foresee the near disaster looming.

Just before she was to leave on a flight for California and the Breeders' Cup Juvenile Fillies at Santa Anita Park, Personal Ensign breezed five furlongs at Belmont — a half-hour later, she could not walk.

X-rays revealed a fracture of the long pastern bone in her left hind leg. Dr. Larry Bramlage of Lexington's Rood & Riddle Equine Hospital flew to

Trainer Shug McGaughey and Personal Ensign

New York and operated on the filly, inserting five stainless steel screws to hold the fracture together.

McGaughey was convinced she would never race again. But, surprising him even more than she had as a juvenile, Personal Ensign recovered under his meticulous care over the following eleven months and was deemed strong enough to return to competition. Indeed, she won all four of her starts as a three-year-old in a two-month span in September

D. Wayne Lukas and Winning Colors, whom the trainer selected at the Keeneland July yearling sale in 1986

and October, including the grade I Beldame Stakes over older fillies and mares. Displaying both grit and resilience, Personal Ensign trounced multiple grade I winner Coup de Fusil by 2¼ lengths over the Beldame's 1¼ miles only eight days after winning the grade II Rare Perfume Stakes at one mile.

Meanwhile, less than a month before Personal Ensign returned to victory as a three-year-old in September 1987, Winning Colors was unfurled at Saratoga Race Course, where she defeated eventual champion Epitome in a seven-furlong maiden race for juvenile fillies.

Lukas, who admitted the filly made his heart hammer when he saw her for the first time at the Keeneland sale, did not press Winning Colors for the Breeders' Cup, an event both she and Personal

Ensign skipped that year. Both Lukas and Mc-Gaughey seemed to know, or at least hope, that better things were in store if they were patient.

Winning Colors started once more as a two-year-old, winning a six-furlong allowance at Santa Anita Park two days after Christmas in a flashy 1:09⅘.

When 1988 began, Winning Colors was stabled on the West Coast and Personal Ensign on the East Coast, again representing different ends of the spectrum.

Winning Colors reeled off an easy win in the La Centinela Stakes at Santa Anita to begin her season in January, lost the grade I Las Virgenes Stakes by just a neck to Goodbye Halo in what Lukas said was the result of overconfidence on his part and too little training, then cruised to an eight-length win in the Santa Anita Oaks over Jeanne Jones and Good-bye Halo. It was then that Lukas decided to really test this roan streak of a filly.

Dispatching her against colts in the Santa Anita Derby, he admitted he was surprised — but only "a little bit" — when she romped home in a tour-de-force of speed, defeating Lively One by 7½ lengths.

"She's a monster!" yelled Klein in the winner's circle. "Kentucky, here we come!"

The former owner of the San Diego Chargers, from whose uniforms the lightning bolt was derived for his silks, Klein had quickly risen to the top of racing after meeting Lukas at Del Mar in 1982 through former Chicago Bears linebacker Dick Butkus.

With Lukas as "coach" of the operation, Klein built a huge stable that he said cost him $300,000 a month to operate. The rewards were great, however, including Eclipse Awards in 1985, '86, and '87 as outstanding owner, and the glory of campaigning 1986 Horse of the Year Lady's Secret and other champions.

Breeders' Cup Distaff
Purse: $1,000,000

6th Race   Churchill Downs - November 5, 1988
Purse $1,000,000. Fillies and mares. Three-year-olds and upward. 1-1/8 Miles. Main Track. Track: Muddy.
Total purse, $1,000,000. Value of race, $913,000. Value to winner $450,000; second, $225,000; third, $108,000; fourth, $70,000; fifth, $50,000; sixth, $10,000. Foal awards, $43,500. Stallion awards, $43,500. Mutuel pool $744,804.

P#	Horse	A	Wgt	Med	Eqp	Odds	PP	St	1/4	1/2	3/4	Str	Fin	Jockey
6	Personal Ensign	4	123			.50	6	8	6^1	$5^{1/2}$	5^2	$3^{1½}$	1no	R P Romero
8	Winning Colors	3	119			b-4.00	8	2	$1^{2½}$	$1^{2½}$	$1^{2½}$	$1^{1½}$	$2^{1/2}$	G L Stevens
2	Goodbye Halo	3	119			5.50	2	1	$2^{1/2}$	3^4	$2^{1/2}$	$2^{2½}$	3^5	E Delahoussaye
3	Sham Say	3	119		b	30.60	3	7	5^2	2^{hd}	3^4	4^1	4^2	J Vasquez
9	Classic Crown	3	119		b	b-4.00	9	5	8^6	7^1	6^5	5^5	5^4	A Cordero Jr
4	Hail a Cab	5	123			a-10.30	4	9	9	9	7^1	7^2	6^2	C J McCarron
1	Epitome	3	119			a-10.30	1	4	$7^{1/2}$	8^5	8^2	8^6	$7^{1/2}$	P Day
5	Willa On the Move	3	119			22.20	5	3	$4^{1/2}$	4^2	4^1	6^{hd}	8^9	C Perret
7	Integra	4	123			83.30	7	6	3^1	6^{hd}	9	9	9	J Velasquez

a-Coupled: Hail a Cab and Epitome; b-Winning Colors and Classic Crown.

Off Time: 3:18   **Time Of Race:** :24⅖   :47⅖   1:12   1:38⅕   1:52
Start: Good For All   **Track:** Muddy

Mutuel Payoffs

6	Personal Ensign	$3.00	$2.20	$2.10
8	Winning Colors (b-entry)		2.80	2.20
3	Goodbye Halo			2.40

Winner: Personal Ensign, b. f, by Private Account—Grecian Banner, by Hoist the Flag (Trained by Claude McGaughey III).
Bred by Ogden Phipps in Ky.

Start good. Won driving.
PERSONAL ENSIGN, caught in close quarters between horses racing to the first turn, commenced to rally after going six furlongs, angled out approaching the stretch and finished determinedly to wear down WINNING COLORS in the final stride. WINNING COLORS sprinted away soon after the start, raced well out from the rail while making the pace, settled into the stretch with a clear advantage and just failed to last. GOODBYE HALO moved to the outside of WINNING COLORS while racing forwardly into the backstretch, remained a factor to the stretch and continued on gamely while drifting out slightly into PERSONAL ENSIGN during the late stages. SHAM SAY edged out into PERSONAL ENSIGN racing to the first turn, remained well out from the rail while racing forwardly to the upper stretch and gave way. CLASSIC CROWN, outrun for six furlongs, moved a little closer along the inside nearing midstretch but lacked a further response. HAIL A CAB was always outrun. EPITOME saved ground to no avail. WILLA ON THE MOVE tired badly while racing wide. INTEGRA showed brief speed while racing wide.

Owners: (6) O Phipps; (8) E V Klein; (2) Campbell Jr & Hancock III; (3) Evergreen Farms; (9) Star Crown Stable; (4) J A Bell III; (1) J A Bell III; (5) R Lamarque; (7) G J Aubin lessee
Trainers: (6) Claude McGaughey III; (8) D Wayne Lukas; (2) Charles Whittingham; (3) William B Cocks; (9) D Wayne Lukas; (4) Philip Hauswald; (1) Philip Hauswald; (5) Leon J Blusiewicz; (7) William R Helmbrecht
©EQUIBASE

Winning Colors would go on to achieve what none of the rest had been able to do — triumph in the Kentucky Derby, only the third filly in history to win the roses and the most recent of the trio including Regret in 1915 and Genuine Risk in 1980.

In another front-running show of power under regular rider Gary Stevens, Winning Colors resolutely defeated Forty Niner by a neck at Churchill Downs, earning the first Derby trophies for Lukas and Stevens as well as for Klein. With television cameras zoomed in on her imposing frame, she rolled out of the far turn with a commanding lead that stretched into immortality.

Her time of 2:02⅕ on a track rated fast was swifter than clockings recorded by such luminary winners as Spectacular Bid, Sunday Silence, Swale, Alysheba, and Silver Charm.

"I've been in sports twenty-five, thirty years, and I've got to say that this is the greatest thrill I've ever had in sports," Klein declared.

Winning Colors went on to be third in Risen Star's Preakness Stakes, after what Klein decried as bullying by Forty Niner and jockey Pat Day, and then last in the Belmont Stakes, also won by Risen Star.

She would not race again until the Maskette Stakes at Belmont on September 10.

Having been rested until May, Personal Ensign continued down her path of perfection, winning the Shuvee and Hempstead handicaps, both grade I races at Belmont, and then the grade II Molly Pitcher Handicap at Monmouth Park in her first racing foray outside of Bemont Park in New York. Phipps, who had raced his first stakes winner in 1935 and had bred and owned such stars as Buckpasser and Numbered Account, flew to Monmouth in a helicopter to watch this special filly, whose tenacity made her his all-time favorite.

As exceptional as she had always been — a virtual racing miracle considering the screws in her leg —

her next race would be one of her career's most pivotal. Running for the first time at Saratoga, she faced males in the historic grade I Whitney Handicap. The fact that only six-time grade I winner Gulch, who would go on to earn champion sprinter honors, and veteran grade I winner King's Swan showed up to take her on was no fault of Personal Ensign's and did not dull the enthusiasm of the 28,756 fans in attendance who made her their strong favorite.

With Gulch, ridden by Jose Santos, setting the pace under only mild pressure from King's Swan and jockey Angel Cordero Jr., Personal Ensign and her regular pilot, Randy Romero, dawdled in the early going, trailing by about three lengths after six furlongs. In a matter of strides, however, Personal Ensign drew even with Gulch coming out of the far turn, and the pair raced together in a determined duel until midstretch. Personal Ensign then began to pull away from the colt, skipping over the finish line with a tired Gulch 1½ lengths behind her.

"I can now say that she is the best I ever rode," Romero said afterward. "I had a lot of horse underneath me, and I wasn't concerned about her getting to [Gulch]."

Lukas, who trained Gulch, contended "it came down to the weight difference," noting that Gulch carried seven more pounds than did Personal Ensign. Yet he conceded, "the filly, let's face it — she's exceptional." Lukas said he was looking forward to a meeting between Winning Colors and Personal Ensign.

Personal Ensign stopped the timer in 1:47⅘, only four-fifths off the stakes and track record that Tri Jet had established in 1974.

"When she kicked in gear on the turn, that's the kind of thing she does so outstandingly," marveled McGaughey, who planned for her next race to be the Ruffian Handicap, named after the legendary filly whose modern mark for distaffers of ten consecutive wins had been tied by Personal Ensign in the Whitney.

Fate would lead McGaughey to change his mind, switching to the weight-for-age Maskette Stakes and a date with Winning Colors on September 10, 1988.

While the one-mile Maskette drew only two other fillies to take on Personal Ensign and Winning Colors, the primary matchup drew plenty of attention as the pair of Amazons prepared to battle. A headline over a commentary in the *New York Times* trumpeted the opinion that "Winning Colors Facing Better Filly in the Maskette" and proclaimed Personal Ensign the best horse in training.

Unfazed by the fact that Winning Colors had not started since her dismal showing in the Belmont Stakes, the worst race of her career, Lukas said she was ready.

As if to demonstrate that fact, Winning Colors shot out of the gate with Stevens in the irons, immediately opening a lead that extended to a nine-length advantage over Personal Ensign at one point in the early going. She was traveling smoothly and appeared to have the race in control; Stevens was thinking her stride felt just as powerful as it did in the Kentucky Derby.

Sitting in his box seat, McGaughey was worried. He had entered Phipps' grade I winner Cadillacing to keep Winning Colors entertained on the lead but then had opted to scratch the full sister to Easy Goer. He was pondering whether he had made a

Personal Ensign made her first foray outside Belmont Park a winning one, taking the Molly Pitcher at Monmouth Park.

serious error when Personal Ensign began her rally, her long bay legs skimming over the track, narrowing the margin with every stride.

Personal Ensign caught Winning Colors and forged ahead in midstretch. Refusing to surrender, the Derby winner fought back, appearing to regain some ground.

As they flashed under the wire, Personal Ensign held a three-quarters-length advantage, with Sham Say third and Thirty Zip the trailer. Returning to be unsaddled, both the bay filly and the roan filly were cheered by the 16,230 fans who knew they had witnessed an epic struggle.

Admitting his concern during the early stages of

Personal Ensign sprinted past the speedy Winning Colors in the weight-for-age Maskette Stakes.

the race, McGaughey noted that Winning Colors was "just galloping, and she wasn't going that fast." In a characteristic understatement that differentiated him from the often bold-talking Lukas, he added, "But my horse is good, and I think, along the way, she has proved a lot."

Both fillies raced again in October, with Person-

al Ensign crushing four opponents to win her second Beldame trophy. Winning Colors, however, faded badly to finish fourth of five in the Spinster Stakes at Keeneland, fifteen lengths behind winner Hail a Cab.

None of that would matter on November 5 when the pair and seven other fillies — all but one a grade I winner — entered the starting gate at Churchill Downs for the $1 million Breeders' Cup Distaff.

Announcer Tom Durkin made clear for the Breeders' Cup record crowd of 71,237 and the NBC television audience what was on the line: "Personal Ensign has taken her place in the starting gate, and she will certainly take her place in history as one of the greatest fillies of all time as she seeks to retire here undefeated, the first major American horse to do so in eighty years."

The day was dreary, cold, and wet, with the track officially labeled muddy. Romero heard Durkin and a thump of the pressure struck his heart as he sat atop the odds-on favorite.

Winning Colors, who had dragged two handlers over to the saddling area, appearing ready to explode, bounded out of the gate. With Stevens riding masterfully, she established an uncontested lead and kept it through easy fractions of :24⅕, 47⅘, and 1:12.

Trying to gain traction on the slippery surface, Personal Ensign seemed to be floundering along toward the inside, about nine lengths behind after a half-mile. Phipps and McGaughey watched with grim faces; their hopes of getting Personal Ensign home to Claiborne with an unblemished racing record seeming to turn to ash in the wake of the roan fireball who was burning up the track on which she had made history six months earlier.

After six furlongs of the 1⅛-mile contest, Romero swung Personal Ensign to the outside as the field turned into the last quarter-mile, and she seemed

Though seemingly beaten, Personal Ensign rallied in the final yards to nip Winning Colors at the wire in the 1988 Breeders' Cup Distaff.

suddenly to come alive, although still four lengths behind at the stretch call. Goodbye Halo had ranged up to within 1½ lengths of Winning Colors and was inching closer in second, and Stevens was riding for the wire, using his whip with his left hand.

Romero urged Personal Ensign forward with the whip in his right hand, and she kept coming, yet it seemed there was no way she could make up the ground. With a sixteenth of a mile to go, she was still several lengths behind the Derby winner although Durkin shouted that she was "uncorking a furious run on the outside."

With Winning Colors resolute and Personal En-

sign relentless, the two fillies came together, the bay streaked with mud and the roan gritting her teeth. The chestnut Goodbye Halo was between them, giving all she had just to keep up.

Only in the final stride did Personal Ensign thrust her nose in front, refusing to be beaten. She crossed the finish line and the threshold into greatness in 1:52. Virtually every person at Churchill Downs that afternoon stood to salute her, with even hardened gamblers in the press box brushing tears from their eyes. It was impossible not to be moved by the virtuosity of the Derby winner and the perfection and determination of her conqueror.

Romero held up his index finger and grinned with a mixture of awe and relief as he rode Personal Ensign back under a thunderous downpour of applause from the grandstand. She had raced thirteen times and had won all thirteen, the first major runner since Colin in 1908 to retire undefeated.

"I thought she was hopelessly beaten at the eighth pole," McGaughey told NBC. His face in the official winner's circle photo reveals how stunned he was by the experience.

"I still don't know how she won," he said later. "To come from where she did with the kind of trip and the conditions, it was really something. Courage, I guess. She won on courage."

In an equal measure of praise, Lukas called Winning Colors' gallant effort the best of her career. He congratulated McGaughey, and both trainers knew that their horses had given them — and racing fans everywhere — the kind of moment they worked their whole lives for, the kind of moment that would last forever.

Epilogue

Following their distinguished 1988 campaigns, Winning Colors and Personal Ensign were declared champions of the three-year-old filly and older filly and mare divisions, respectively. Phipps, who also had been represented that year by juvenile champion Easy Goer and other grade I winners Seeking the Gold, Mining, and Personal Ensign's full brother Personal Flag, won Eclipse Awards as outstanding owner and breeder.

Personal Ensign went on to be just as dazzling a producer as she was a racehorse. Her foals included grade I winners Miner's Mark, My Flag, and Traditionally, and her son Our Emblem sired Kentucky Derby and Preakness winner War Emblem. She was named Broodmare of the Year in 1996 and then later achieved even more acclaim when her granddaughter Storm Flag Flying emulated her dam My Flag's victory in the Breeders' Cup Juvenile Fillies, forging an unprecedented three-generation Breeders' Cup dynasty for Personal Ensign. In 2006 Personal Ensign was pensioned at Claiborne.

Winning Colors endured some troubles in the breeding shed. As of spring 2008 she is credited with no stakes winners but she did produce the first filly to top the Keeneland July select sale when her daughter by Mr. Prospector brought a bid of $1.05 million in 1994. Winning Colors was euthanized in February 2008 after enduring complications from colic.

Saturday
Afternoon
Showdowns

EASY GOER – SUNDAY SILENCE

BY GARY WEST

F or many, they defined racing. Their meetings lifted racing to a place rarely seen anymore, to an arena of idealized and rarified competition. They confronted each other time and again on the sport's largest stage, and their confrontations brought out a throng of fans, a multitude of television viewers, and, of course, a host of clichés: They were as good as it gets, they were what it was all about, and, yes, they represented racing at its best.

Clichés, however, are inadequate to describe those meetings of Sunday Silence and Easy Goer. For most of 1989, they were the two best horses in the country, and perhaps the world. But by any measure they were also two of the best horses of the era, both destined for the Hall of Fame. If not for the other, either would have swept the Triple Crown.

Sunday Silence and Easy Goer turned for home in a thrilling Preakness Stakes.

Sunday Silence stunned Easy Goer fans with his Kentucky Derby victory.

But their four meetings represented more than the inevitable clashing of superlative talents, more than televised spectacle, more even than championships. Their confrontations sparkled with metaphorical implications, for these two champions, a sleek black colt from the West and a powerful chestnut from the East, were in many ways opposites, compellingly drawn together by the Triple Crown, the Breeders' Cup, and, most of all, the unifying pursuit of greatness.

Easy Goer

From the start, expectations soared. Easy Goer had the pedigree and the looks that inevitably encourage lofty hopes and roseate dreams. And as his trainer, Claude "Shug" McGaughey, explains, the colt suggested with all his training in the mornings, with each spin around the track, with every gallop and workout, that he possessed uncommon ability.

Absolutely everything about Easy Goer was regal, from his provenance to his potential. By Alydar, the co-star in Affirmed's Triple Crown, and out of the champion mare Relaxing, Easy Goer was bred and owned by Ogden Phipps, a founding member of the New York Racing Association and chairman of The Jockey Club. The colt was born and raised at the famed Claiborne Farm near Paris, Kentucky.

Phipps had raced such champions as Buckpasser, Numbered Account, Queen of the Stage, Vitriolic, and, of course, Relaxing. The patriarch of New York racing owned the great sire Bold Ruler. And if, as part of a foal-sharing agreement, a coin had flipped a little differently, Phipps would have owned the glorious result of that 1969 mating of Bold Ruler and Somethingroyal. In other words, because of a coin flip, he owned The Bride instead of her full brother, Secretariat.

But for a while in 1988 and 1989, it looked as if

fate had flipped the coin again, and to Phipps' favor this time. Easy Goer was so conspicuously talented, so flashy and dominant in spite of troublesome ankles, that not only did he invite comparisons to the 1973 Triple Crown winner, but he seemed to insist upon them.

Like Secretariat, Easy Goer had a troubled trip and lost his debut, rallying to finish second by a nose. And like Secretariat, after his initial setback, Easy Goer for a time seemed invincible. An easy maiden win at Saratoga led to an even easier allowance victory at Belmont Park, where he then won the Cowdin Stakes by three lengths and the Champagne Stakes by four, and he did it all with aplomb, leaving onlookers stunned and handicappers dazzled.

Easy Goer already was performing on a level that only the best older horses ever reached. In the Champagne, for example, he moved through an opening along the rail at the top of the Belmont stretch and ran the last quarter-mile, while hand-ridden to the wire, in about 24⅗ seconds, completing the mile in 1:34⅘. Moments after the race his jockey, Pat Day, pronounced Easy Goer to be the most impressive two-year-old he had ever ridden. In truth, Easy Goer was probably the most impressive two-year-old anybody had ridden since, well, Secretariat.

 With his reputation growing and the comparisons swirling, Easy Goer went to the Breeders' Cup championships at Churchill Downs. This was a heady time for the sport, a time of ripened anticipation. The day itself was wet and dreary and cold, but that couldn't dampen the expectations or diminish the significance of the racing. With a victory in the Breeders' Cup Distaff over Kentucky Derby winner Winning Colors, Personal Ensign could retire undefeated; with a victory in the Breeders' Cup Classic, Alysheba could retire as the sport's all-time leading

money winner. On the grandstand apron, picking up the year's political theme, a banner urged "Alysheba For President."

While many that day at Churchill wanted, however jokingly, Alysheba for their next president, many more wanted Easy Goer for their next superhorse. Or, at least, they expected such an outcome: He was the 3-10 favorite in the Juvenile.

But Easy Goer didn't run as he had in his previous four outings. Bumped around at the start of the Juvenile, he dropped back to seventh, raced wide and never seemed to find his stride until the stretch, and even there, having never raced around two turns before, he jumped over the tracks left by the starting gate. He finished second, more than a length behind Is It True, whom he had soundly defeated in the Champagne.

"He just didn't have any confidence in his footing," Day explained, attributing the loss to the muddy track condition and comparing Easy Goer's tentative running to a person's walking gingerly on ice. "He got bumped, and he was climbing down the backstretch," Day said. "He finished second without ever getting out of second gear."

From racetrack to racetrack, surfaces differ, of course, even saturated surfaces, and no two muddy tracks are exactly alike. The mud at Churchill, Day said, can be like peanut butter. And Easy Goer didn't like peanut butter.

Still, the big chestnut was named the year's champion juvenile. The Breeders' Cup loss, because of the track condition, did little damage to his reputation. And if there had been any doubt about him, even a soupçon of suspicion about his talent, he quickly dispelled it the following season with his performances in the Swale and the Gotham.

Easy Goer began his 1989 campaign in Florida, rallying outside from fifth to win the Swale Stakes by nearly nine lengths. But that was just a prelude.

He then won the Gotham Stakes at Aqueduct by thirteen, breaking Secretariat's stakes record by a full second, setting a track record and nearly equaling the world record. And Day didn't use his whip in either race. It was all Easy Goer and his massive talent, all about a big red train, rolling toward Kentucky.

That Gotham still stands out in Day's mind as perhaps the greatest performance by the greatest horse he ever rode. "He made a couple of different moves in the race," Day said, referring to Easy Goer's sudden advance down the backstretch and then to the colt's knockout punch in the lane. "He was certainly on his game that day. He was running, but he wasn't all out. He wasn't straining significantly underneath me."

Easy Goer completed the mile in 1:32⅖, just a tick, a mere length, off Dr. Fager's world record set in 1968. And Easy Goer wasn't even straining; he was just rolling.

The Wood Memorial produced more of the same, but the fireworks weren't quite as bright or as thunderous as they had been in the Gotham. Easy Goer stalked the pace, effortlessly took control, and won, with little encouragement, by three lengths, and then, just to add the necessary punctuation, he galloped out strongly, leaving the others — they were hardly "rivals" — far behind. By Easy Goer standards and expectations, the performance wasn't spectacular, but it seemed to be the perfect preparatory tune-up for Kentucky.

An Interlude

Maybe it was in October, or it could have been November 1988, but the date hardly matters. The memory remains forever vivid for Arthur Hancock III, even if the date isn't.

One day at Louie's Restaurant in Paris, Kentucky, as he recalls it, he bumped into his brother, Seth. They chatted awhile, and talk turned, as it eventually must in Kentucky, to horses.

"It looks like we got a real nice colt out in California," Arthur Hancock said.

"That's too bad," Seth Hancock told his older brother, "because I hear Mr. Phipps has the best horse he's ever bred."

Sunday Silence

Nobody wanted Sunday Silence except Arthur Hancock III. That's the simple truth of it. Bred by Oak Cliff Thoroughbreds, Sunday Silence was born at Hancock's Stone Farm near Paris, Kentucky, and nearly died from a viral infection before his first birthday.

When he was offered at auction as a yearling, specifically at the Keeneland July sale of 1987, he attracted no buyers, and so for $17,000 Hancock brought him back to Stone Farm. The following year Hancock tried to sell the colt again, sending him to California, but with a similar result. Hancock bought him back, this time for $32,000.

Sunday Silence had an attractive pedigree, by Halo out of Wishing Well. The winner of the United Nations Handicap, Halo already had established himself as a successful stallion, with such horses as Devil's Bag and Sunny's Halo. And Wishing Well was a multiple stakes winner of $381,625.

But apparently Sunday Silence himself wasn't very attractive. The colt was tall and "gangly," Hancock said, and cow-hocked. On one bloodstock agent's personal graded scale of assessment, the colt was a triple-zero, which must have been a tripod intended to support heavy disapproval.

And then there was the accident. As a two-year-old, Sunday Silence was in a van that overturned when the driver had a heart attack. Everything, in other words, about the young colt was either discouraging or disappointing.

Sunday Silence and Easy Goer ran in unison the length of the stretch of an epic Preakness battle.

But then he ran, and by running he defined himself in ways that had nothing to do with being unattractive or unwanted. He defined himself as a racehorse.

"This big black sonofabitch can run a little bit," Charlie Whittingham told Hancock one morning by telephone, referring to the two-year-old that had been left behind with the Hall of Fame trainer after not selling at auction.

That, Hancock said, was the first thing Whittingham ever told him about the horse. And in typical Whittingham fashion, the comment was an understatement: The black colt could run a little indeed.

How much he could run wouldn't be clear for a while. Like Easy Goer, Sunday Silence finished second in his first outing but probably should have won. Losing by a neck, he raced greenly, and in doing so he revealed a reluctance to keep a straight course in the stretch. It was a reluctance that would resurface.

But this was a time for education, and in his next outing, Sunday Silence won by ten lengths. He then completed his juvenile campaign by finishing second in an allowance affair, a head behind the highly regarded Houston. But once again, Sunday Silence ran somewhat erratically in the stretch.

Sunday Silence began his three-year-old season in March with a facile victory over a sloppy Santa Anita surface, and seventeen days later, in the San Felipe, he made his stakes debut. He had run four times, and although he twice had lost in a photo finish, he probably should have been unbeaten.

Nevertheless, he never had raced around two turns or in stakes company, nor did he bring a huge reputation into the race, and so he wasn't the bettors' favorite in the San Felipe. That role went to Music Merci, who just had won the San Rafael Stakes by nine lengths.

But Music Merci couldn't match Sunday Silence, who in the San Felipe implied that he, too, might be rolling toward Kentucky. After an awkward start, Sunday Silence quickly put himself in a prominent stalking position. He dragged jockey Pat Valenzuela to the lead in the second turn and then powered through the stretch to win by nearly two lengths over Flying Continental. And then, in the Santa Anita Derby, Sunday Silence issued a loud and reverberating challenge.

Ever since he sold for $2.9 million as a yearling, Houston was marked for stardom. He won his debut by 12½ lengths, ran down Sunday Silence to win his second outing and then went to New York to win the Bay Shore Stakes by 10½. He returned to the West Coast as a headliner and the unbeaten favorite for the 1989 Santa Anita Derby.

But, of course, Sunday Silence stole the show. Houston and Sunday Silence, side by side in the gate, came together and bumped at the start. Houston recovered quickly enough, however, to assume the lead as the field entered the first turn, with Sunday Silence stalking, a couple lengths back in third.

Sunday Silence had a remarkable talent for running the turn. His extraordinary athleticism enabled him to alter his stride in a blink, changing leads and leaning aggressively into the turn with his left foreleg. Unlike other horses, he didn't have to slow down to get around a turn, explained jockey Chris McCarron, who would ride him later that year. To some it seemed as if Sunday Silence could actually accelerate through the turn, and maybe he could, for he certainly enjoyed his greatest advantage there. In the turn, he won many of his races.

And it was in the second turn that he took control of the Santa Anita Derby. With Valenzuela sitting motionless, Sunday Silence swirled around the second turn, running to and quickly by Music Merci and Houston. They capitulated without argument. In the stretch Sunday Silence ducked in when Valenzuela hit him right-handed; but then the black colt straightened and drew away powerfully and dominantly, winning by eleven lengths and completing the 1⅛ miles in 1:47⅗, or three lengths off the stakes record.

In the very next moment, on the nationally televised broadcast of the race, a camera focused on Whittingham, looking not so much celebratory as intensely earnest while making his way to the winner's circle, and racing sportscaster Dave Johnson commented that the "Bald Eagle," as the venerable trainer was called, had one eye on Kentucky and the other on Easy Goer.

The Derby

The public was much more sanguine than most of the participants. The bettors made Easy Goer, along with his stablemate Awe Inspiring, their 4-5 favorite in the 115th Kentucky Derby. Sunday Silence they respected, at 3-1. A victory by anybody else was beyond the reach of even the wildest imagination.

McGaughey had seen Sunday Silence's romp at Santa Anita, and so he wasn't nearly as confident as the bettors. Sunday Silence, he knew, would be tough to beat. And Day was concerned because of the weather. Rain fell on Louisville, and the temperature dipped into the forties, a record low for Derby Day. Although the rain had stopped its onslaught by post time, the track for the Derby was officially muddy, with puddles of water for emphasis. Yes, it was very much like that day six months earlier when Easy Goer had finished second in the Breeders' Cup Juvenile.

Although Sunday Silence had won a race on a sloppy track, Hancock wasn't confident either. He had confidence in his horse, but he didn't expect to win the Derby, not really, not in any anticipatory way, because he had come to expect disappointment, regarding it as inevitable when confronted with such forces as these.

In 1972, when A.B. "Bull" Hancock died, the advisers to his estate recommended to the board of directors that leadership of Claiborne Farm be turned over to Seth Hancock rather than to his older brother. And the most influential of those advisers was Ogden Phipps.

The following year Arthur Hancock left Claiborne to establish Stone Farm. And so the confrontation and the rivalry, along with the inevitability of disappointment, all reached back into the histories of the families, their farms, and their horses. The rivalry reached down deeply, too, into a turbulence of hopes, dreams, and aspirations. All of this converged in a sort of mythic confluence on this day and with this Derby, as, the fanciful might say, fate surely intended.

Only Whittingham was confident. He had become a partner in Sunday Silence, along with Ernest Gaillard, a California physician and Louisville native. Forever astute and seldom given to pronouncements, Whittingham said flatly and unequivocally that Sunday Silence would win.

And, of course, he was right.

Bumped at the start and then steadied, Sunday Silence, nevertheless, found a perfect position in fourth as the field of fifteen straightened for the run down the backstretch. Houston led through lively fractions, followed by Clever Trevor and Northern Wolf. Sunday Silence seemed to be moving easily, and to his outside in fifth ran Easy Goer.

Down the backstretch, it became apparent that Easy Goer wasn't himself. Day nudged him along but got little response. In the second turn, without much urging, Sunday Silence advanced. He struck the front as the field turned into the stretch. Valenzuela encouraged him with a right-handed stick, and Sunday Silence ducked in, brushing with Northern Wolf; the jockey switched the stick to his left hand, and the black colt ducked out.

Sunday Silence came down the Churchill stretch like a well-oiled reveler on New Year's Eve, ducking in and then out and then in again. Somehow, though, he avoided disaster, largely because nobody else was running much at the time. Sunday Silence won by 2½ lengths, completing the 1¼ miles in a modest 2:05; Easy Goer rallied to finish second without threatening, a head in front of his stablemate.

The Kentucky Derby, as it turned out, reiterated the known and confirmed the suspected: Sunday Silence and Easy Goer were the best three-year-olds in the country, and one of them didn't especially care for the mud at Churchill Downs. Beyond that, though, questions remained. They waited for a race that many still regard as one of the best of the era.

The Preakness

On the morning of the race, Hancock read that ninety-seven of one hundred Turf writers covering the Preakness were picking Easy Goer to win. This worried Hancock, for he knew the mud had played a part in Sunday Silence's victory in Kentucky. Most of all, though, it worried him that his horse wasn't receiving the proper respect due a Derby winner. And so Hancock took the information to Whittingham, just down the hall in the same Baltimore hotel.

"Those sports writers," Whittingham said, as Hancock recalls it, "don't even know what color your horse is."

And just as Whittingham finished his assessment of sports writers in general and ninety-seven of them in particular, one of them appeared on the nearby television screen to say, "Few of the experts give the son of Halo a chance in today's Preakness."

"That's when I knew we were going to win," Hancock said.

Despite the Derby, Easy Goer was the 3-5 favorite.

Easy Goer relished the sweeping turns of Belmont Park to exact his revenge in the third leg of the Triple Crown.

After all, the track was fast, and many still expected him to become the next superhorse, even if he wouldn't have a Triple Crown to brandish. As flaws went, a disdain for mud was so minor that it could be excused, especially in a superstar.

The record crowd at Pimlico — 90,145 — made Sunday Silence 2-1 but remained, like at least ninety-seven sports writers, somewhat skeptical. After all, Sunday Silence had missed a couple days of training with a minor foot problem, and he had shown a propensity for imitating at times a drunken reveler. Valenzuela had explained the colt's weaving through the stretch at Churchill Downs by saying it was a reaction to the Derby throng. But that explanation didn't play well in Baltimore, or anywhere else; Sunday Silence had seen some erratic moments even before Kentucky.

But all the expectations and concerns and skepticism faded into the background once the 114th Preakness began. Sunday Silence ran in fourth as the field of eight entered the first turn, with Easy Goer just behind him. They had perfect positions, and as they advanced down the backstretch, gaining on the leaders, they became the race, clearly and entirely.

Concerned he would get floated wide, Day loosened his hold on Easy Goer, who shot forward, first passing Sunday Silence and then Houston, the early leader. Easy Goer took a narrow lead into the second turn. And there, Day recalled, he "let him down a little bit," giving the colt a momentary breather.

"But just that quick, Sunday Silence was back on us," Day said, as if still surprised and eternally impressed with the suddenness of it all. Sunday Silence again used the turn to his advantage.

He grabbed the lead with a quarter-mile remaining, and Easy Goer, who didn't get a breather after all, tried to fight back on the inside. And together, eyeball to eyeball with matched determination, they ran the length of the Pimlico stretch.

Easy Goer had won the Swale, the Gotham, and the Wood by rallying outside of horses, and now he suddenly and unexpectedly found himself pinned down on the rail. It was, Day remembered, an uncomfortable position for the red colt.

Still, Easy Goer gamely came back, putting his head in front in deep stretch, and then Sunday Silence returned the fight: A puncher and a boxer, they fought determinedly to the wire, the puncher landing some big blows but then missing some others, and the boxer countering and jabbing, all the while the two of them circling and looking for an opening, for a knockout, which, of course, never came because, well, they were just too good.

"Sunday Silence had been leaning on me," Day said, recalling the final strides of the Preakness, where he tried to resist the outside pressure. But Easy Goer could turn only his head; his body was too spent to follow.

Nine times with a right-handed whip, Valenzuela entreated Sunday Silence for more effort, and the black colt responded, bearing in and bearing down and finally winning by a nose in the closest Preakness ever run.

They completed the 1³⁄₁₆ miles in 1:53⅖, the third-fastest clocking in the history of the race. Day objected, claiming foul and alleging interference in the stretch. But after several minutes the stewards made it official: Sunday Silence had won two-thirds of the Triple Crown.

The Belmont

After the Preakness, McGaughey said he expected to hear all the Affirmed-Alydar comparisons. And they would be endless, with Easy Goer eternally locked into the role of runner-up, if in the Belmont Stakes he again finished second and if Sunday Silence became the sport's twelfth Triple Crown winner. But, of course, McGaughey had three weeks to make sure that didn't happen.

In many ways the Preakness was more disappointing for him than the Derby had been. The muddy surface explained the loss in Kentucky. Easy Goer had no such excuse in Maryland.

On the other hand, McGaughey said, the Preakness convinced him that Easy Goer could indeed beat his rival. Only a nose, after all, separated them. Inches really. And both trainer and jockey believed then, as they believe now, that Easy Goer would have won the Preakness had he been outside of Sunday Silence rather than pinned on the rail.

So maybe a different strategy would produce a different outcome. Or maybe the distance would, the famous 1½ miles that, some say fondly, tests champions. And if not the distance, then surely the track itself would alter the dynamic and tip the scales, for Belmont Park's vast oval and sweeping turns would minimize any advantage in athleticism that Sunday Silence might have.

And then, the night before the Belmont Stakes, torrential rains fell on Long Island. Belmont Park closed its track to training the next morning, and it seemed Easy Goer would surely face another muddy surface.

But the sun, which had been so bashful all week, suddenly burst through to make a bright appearance early in the day. And the surface dried so quickly that it was pronounced "fast" long before post time. Could it be that circumstances so abruptly shifted allegiance?

Or was Easy Goer just unbeatable that day? Oddly enough, for the first time in the Triple Crown, he wasn't the betting favorite. Easy Goer's odds were 8-5.

Sunday Silence's were 4-5. In a field with little early speed, the Halo could control the pace to his advantage, or at least that was the most probable

scenario, but even that changed suddenly and unexpectedly when Le Voyageur, an unlikely invader from France, went for the lead out of the gate. With Sunday Silence stalking, Le Voyageur took the field of ten through an opening half-mile in forty-seven seconds and six furlongs in 1:11⅕, lively splits for such a distance.

In the second turn, Sunday Silence made his move and briefly put his head in front. But on the outside, Easy Goer moved, too. And he moved irresistibly.

Easy Goer went by so quickly, he looked like a train Sunday Silence had just missed. And Sunday Silence had no response, not this time. Easy Goer pushed his advantage to four lengths, six lengths, eight lengths at the finish, stopping the teletimer at 2:26, the second-fastest clocking in Belmont history.

Rivalry Redux

Although second in New York, Sunday Silence won a million-dollar bonus for the best performance in the Triple Crown series. That was $2.5 million shy of what it might have been with a Belmont victory. Still, he had two gems, which would suffice most seasons to win the golden Eclipse Award symbolic of the Horse of the Year.

Strangely enough, though, by November, Sunday Silence was again in the position of having to prove himself. In his post-Belmont return, he finished second in the Swaps Stakes at Hollywood Park, surrendering a four-length lead to Prized in deep stretch. And although Sunday Silence won the Super Derby at Louisiana Downs by six lengths, the victory hardly matched the accomplishments piling high for Easy Goer.

The loss in the Preakness, McGaughey said, had made Easy Goer a better horse, and he seemed to prove it with each outing. After the Belmont he defeated older horses in the Whitney Handicap at Saratoga, where two weeks later he won the Travers Stakes. He even won in the mud, beating older horses in the Woodward Handicap at Belmont before handily winning the Jockey Club Gold Cup.

Easy Goer and Sunday Silence had proven themselves, and they had proven themselves against each other. But there could be only one Horse of the Year and that would be the winner of the Breeders' Cup Classic at Gulfstream Park.

Easy Goer was again the bettors' favorite, at 1-2, with Sunday Silence at 2-1. But the situation had changed since their Triple Crown confrontations. Valenzuela had been suspended. And so Chris McCarron, who never had ridden the horse in the afternoon, had the mount on Sunday Silence for the Breeders' Cup.

"I was confident that I was on a horse that could beat Easy Goer," McCarron said, putting some topspin on "could," as if to suggest he was also aware of a horse that could beat Sunday Silence. But he also knew Sunday Silence was training "as well as a horse could possibly train."

Before the Breeders' Cup Sunday Silence had strung together several impressive workouts, including a mile at Del Mar in 1:33⅖, which McCarron still remembers as "unbelievable." And after the Super Derby victory Whittingham had pronounced the colt to be "ready for Easy Goer."

But the Bald Eagle made no predictions as he had at Churchill Downs. The rivalry had gone beyond that. Everything had been said, the compliments paid, the respect given. Only their final confrontation remained, and, in the end, it would only con-

Sunday Silence made it 3-1 in the 1989 Breeders' Cup Classic at Gulfstream Park.

EASY GOER – SUNDAY SILENCE

firm that they both were superlative.

From the inside post position, Easy Goer came away from the gate awkwardly, and then he ducked inward as he left the chute, at that point where it and the stretch and the turn all intersected.

"His mind was a million miles away," Day said, recalling the start of the Classic.

And so after a half-mile in 46⅕ seconds, Easy Goer was six lengths behind Sunday Silence, who was third, and eleven lengths behind the leader, Slew City Slew. Down the backstretch Sunday Silence settled into his long-striding rhythm and advanced to within four lengths of the lead. Easy Goer advanced, too, moving strongly to get within a length of Sunday Silence as the field approached the second turn. And for an instant the Classic looked like the Preakness, but the supporting cast at Gulfstream still had some meaningful lines.

Blushing John, who would be named the year's champion older horse, became the new leader in the second turn. As always, Sunday Silence did some of best work there, and when they straightened for the run down the lane, he was at Blushing John's hip. And he kept coming. In midstretch, with McCarron prudently shunning the whip, Sunday Silence drew alongside the leader, clearly on his way to grabbing the advantage for his own.

Easy Goer, however, had dropped back in the turn, leaving himself with a deficit of 4½ lengths in the stretch. But then, switching to his right lead, he charged again, bursting toward the wire, dropping his belly and reaching for real estate. Just as Sunday Silence seemed certain to win, Easy Goer seemed determined to prevent his rival's victory.

Sunday Silence won by a neck, completing the 1¼ miles in 2:00⅕. Most of all, though, they finished together.

Epilogue

Sunday Silence and Easy Goer were expected to face each other again the following year, in a million-dollar extravaganza at Arlington, a race created especially to accommodate their rivalry. Injuries, however, forced both into retirement before they could meet.

Sunday Silence won nine of his fourteen races, with five seconds, and he earned $4,968,554 in his career. Easy Goer won fourteen of twenty, with five seconds and a third, and he earned $4,873,770.

Sunday Silence, of course, won three of their four meetings. Easy Goer's single victory over Sunday Silence, however, was dominant. And so their fans and supporters still argue.

But perhaps McGaughey has the correct perspective: Quite simply, Easy Goer and Sunday Silence were each capable of beating the other. "To be able to get through the Triple Crown," he said, "and accomplish what they accomplished throughout the year, they were both great horses."

And they had a great rivalry.

189

Racing's Silver Comets

BY LENNY SHULMAN

As Free House and Silver Charm thundered down the stretch of the 1997 Preakness Stakes without a matchbox's worth of space between them, photographer Skip Dickstein's camera shutter clicked, freezing in time the two great grays digging in with all they had, clods of the Pimlico track flying in their wake.

Free House, he of the dramatic bright gray coat and even bolder white blaze across his face, is flashing his hot, black right eye in a showdown stare toward his rival. Silver Charm, head cocked ever so slightly in the direction of his familiar foe, checks out Free House's proximity with his left eyeball.

In eight races played out over three years, this is how it was between them — matching strides in a bid for glory. Their confronta-

The 1997 Preakness showcased the last great rivalry of the twentieth century, the one between Silver Charm and Free House, on the rail.

tions, sadly, could well be the last of their kind for quite some time. Given the vast choice of races and venues, and horsemen's inclination to find the easiest spots for their budding or current stars, nobody is looking to butt heads as this pair did, in a half-dozen consecutive races during their three-year-old campaigns alone.

Since their matchups of the late 1990s, no rivalry has come close to challenging this pair of fighters, ready to answer the bell at each ringing. They brought the finest facets of racing history alive in their battles. Almost 37,000 fortunate fans were at Santa Anita Park when they hooked up in the Santa Anita Derby, the crowd getting to experience what they'd seen in the old newsreels, when

Silver Charm

a sea of suit-and-fedora-wearing fans would rise in waves along the grandstand as the giants of yesteryear screamed past toward the reward of the wire. That was precisely the effect of that 1997 spring day, excitement washing over the crowd as the pair of fan favorites etched themselves into a collective, cherished memory.

The essential part of a great rivalry, of course, is competing against one another repeatedly. But the competition between Silver Charm and Free House had other alluring facets. Each being gray certainly helped. As did both being California based. Neither boasted a pedigree that screamed quality, making them underdogs in the blueblood world of Thoroughbreds.

Then there were the owners. In Silver Charm's camp were Bob and Beverly Lewis, universally admired and applauded for being superior sportspeople willing to give as much back to the game and their community as they received.

Bob Lewis, whose Southern California Anheuser-Busch distributorship made him a wealthy man, and his wife, Beverly, had already enjoyed enormous success in Thoroughbreds through their champion filly Serena's Song. Bob Lewis' gosh-darn demeanor hid a fierce competitive spirit, yet he was always the first to congratulate another winner, even if the victory had come at his expense.

Behind Free House were his Canadian-born breeders and partners Trudy McCaffery and John Toffan. McCaffery's bubbling enthusiasm for the sport was contagious. Before her death in 2007, McCaffery served on various industry and charitable boards. She founded Kids to the Cup, which introduced youngsters to racing. The couple also raced standouts Bien Bien and Came Home.

Both ownership groups respected and liked one another, and a good-natured rivalry formed between them as well as their horses.

Most important, though, the competitive hearts of both horses fueled the rivalry. Said Bob Baffert, Silver Charm's trainer, "What made them so popular is that every time they ran, they just laid it down and put on a show for everybody. I think over time they wore each other out, like Ali and Frazier, and it probably took its toll."

McCaffery and Toffan bought Free House's sire, Smokester, and dam, Fountain Lake, for $35,000 and $40,000, respectively, at the Barretts 1990 spring sale of two-year-olds in training. Fountain Lake went on to become a minor stakes winner, and Smokester took half of his four races before a foot problem led to his retirement.

Free House was born at Cardiff Stud Farm near Creston, California, where he received his first breaking lessons, later shifting over to McCaffery's and Toffan's Eskay Creek Farm near Bradbury, California, for the finishing touches. Named after pubs in the farm country of England (often called free houses), Free House was a free spirit, and a slow learner.

"You could see as a young two-year-old he had great movement," said Toffan. "What held him back was he was a little spooky and had a tendency to duck. But you could see the talent.

"He should have won his first race by ten lengths, but he was in and out and all over the place."

Free House, in the care of trainer Paco Gonzalez, proved victorious in his second race, and in his third outing was good enough to capture the Norfolk Stakes in October 2006. "That was a little bit of a surprise," allowed Toffan, "because he was still learning how to run." After a pair of nondescript stakes losses, Free House was through for the year.

As for Silver Charm, small-time breeder Mary Lou Wootton took her Poker mare, Bonnie's Poker, to Silver Buck in 1993 with no visions of grandeur. "He was the best stallion we could afford, and we owned

Free House

a share in the horse," said her husband, Gordon Wootton. From that mating emerged Silver Charm.

The Woottons sold Silver Charm at an Ocala yearling sale for $16,500 to Randy Hartley and Dean De Renzo, who later sold him privately to Canadian C.J. Gray. Gray subsequently failed to sell Silver Charm at the 1996 Ocala April two-year-olds in training sale. However, the colt had caught the attention of agents J.B. McKathan and Kevin McKathan, who called him "the best horse in the sale." The brothers also had a pipeline to Baffert, and they put the deal together privately for $85,000, hoping Silver Charm would return Baffert to the Triple Crown trail, where he was with Cavonnier at the time they did the deal for Silver Charm.

And that's precisely how it played out. After a runner-up effort in his curtain raiser, Silver Charm

Silver Charm started "goofing off" after gaining the lead, according to jockey Gary Stevens, and barely held off Captain Bodgit.

won his maiden second time out, and, like Free House, annexed a stakes contest in his third test, winning the Del Mar Futurity in September 1996. Hoping to preserve his horse for the rigors ahead, Baffert put him away for the remainder of the season.

In early February 1997, Silver Charm and Free House first met in the San Vicente Stakes at Santa Anita. Free House had run a desultory seventh three weeks earlier in the Golden Gate Derby, and Silver Charm was coming into the San Vicente off a five-month layoff. Both horses gave their connections reasons for doubt and hope.

Baffert was sitting in a box with Beverly Lewis when Silver Charm broke through the gate before the race. "I turned to Beverly and said, 'Forget about it,'" Baffert said. "I'd never had one break through the gate hard and run well. Then, he didn't break well, and he was down on the inside behind horses, and that was a first for him. I was just hoping to light the board."

Silver Charm ended up in a nice spot along the rail while a speed duel played out up front. His rider, Chris McCarron, patiently stayed inside, finally making his move and gaining the lead near the eighth pole. Silver Charm started to draw off.

Free House, under Eddie Delahoussaye, was making heavy weather of it back in the pack. Along the inside early, and ill at ease, Free House responded when moved out for clear running up the backstretch. But he drifted wide turning for home and could only pick up the second spot, 1¾ lengths behind Silver Charm at the wire.

"That race," noted Baffert, "is when I knew I had something special. To come back after that start and run seven furlongs in 1:21 flat, I started getting a little Derby fever."

Toffan was able to see the silver lining for Free House. "He had the talent, but even at three he still had the antics, too. It was just going to be a question of how long before he put it all together."

The wait proved not all that long. Five weeks after the San Vicente, Silver Charm and Free House renewed acquaintances in the 1¹⁄₁₆-mile San Felipe Stakes. Free House had the advantage of already having run four races around two turns while Silver Charm would be trying it for the first time.

Now partnered with David Flores, Free House received his ritual pre-race kiss on the nose from McCaffery, and Flores got him going early, tracking the early pace from second. One of Free House's tricks was turning off his engine once he made the lead, so Flores did not want to turn on the heat too soon. But entering the stretch, he asked Free House for his best, and they made the lead.

Silver Charm, meantime, launched a bid from midpack, picking off foes steadily while gaining on his pal. He moved inexorably closer, but this time Free House kept to his work and hit the wire three-quarters of a length in front of runner-up Silver Charm.

Both camps had reason to be encouraged. It was Free House's first victory in five races since the Norfolk. Moreover, Silver Charm passed the two-turn test with something left in the tank for the next

dance, the Santa Anita Derby three weeks later.

With nothing less than tickets to Louisville at stake, both horses had different riders for Santa Anita's signature three-year-old race. Kent Desormeaux was back aboard Free House for the first time since the previous December, and Gary Stevens mounted Silver Charm. Amazingly, neither gained the status of favorite for the race, that going to Sharp Cat, a Lukas filly with four straight wins in her column. Her speed influenced the way Baffert approached the contest.

"I told Gary before the race I didn't want Sharp Cat to steal away and pull a Winning Colors [front-running victory] on us," said Baffert. "I told him to put the pressure on her."

Following orders, Stevens had Silver Charm lapped onto the filly around the first turn and up the backstretch. Desormeaux, seeing the speed duel unfold, sat just behind and to the outside of that pair as they tore up the backstretch, the first half-mile clicking away in a suicidal :45.

Sharp Cat made six furlongs in 1:09, but entering the turn for home, she'd had enough. Silver Charm inherited a brief advantage, but Free House exploded by like the easiest of winners.

"I figured Silver Charm was empty at that point," Baffert said. "When Free House went by, it looked like he would win by three lengths."

The heart of Silver Charm, however, would not let that happen. Off in their own match race, the pair of grays streaked down the Santa Anita stretch, Silver Charm somehow finding another gear while Free House, outside of him, began to decelerate ever so slightly. Past a grandstand filled with admirers, they moved as one to the wire, with Free House prevailing by a head.

Baffert's post-race comments indicated how the Free House-Silver Charm rivalry had colored his thinking and strategy — not the last time a participant in this head-to-head competition would chalk up a strategic error to the ongoing battle.

"I may have given too much credit to Sharp Cat and not enough to Free House," the trainer admitted. Yet, he preferred to look ahead with positive thoughts. "I had just lost the Santa Anita Derby, but I was so excited my horse didn't pack it in. It was exactly the kind of hard, tough race he needed to set him up perfectly for the Kentucky Derby."

With the California portion of their shared history wrapped up, at least for the time being, the two grays headed for the Triple Crown series, taking their show on the road first to Louisville, where their Golden State clashes didn't quite capture the hearts and minds of Kentucky Derby wagerers. Neither was made the favorite for the Run for the Roses; that privilege belonged to Team Valor's Captain Bodgit, who had done his campaigning on the East Coast, whisking home from off the pace to win the Florida Derby and Wood Memorial.

Both grays settled in at Churchill Downs, despite often wet and chilly weather leading up to the big day. Free House worked well enough, finishing his morning tests with enough vigor to please his connections, who were Derby veterans. Trainer Gonzalez had brought third-place finisher Mane Minister to the 1991 Derby for McCaffery and Toffan.

Baffert, hoping to erase the pain of Cavonnier's nose defeat in the 1996 Derby, made sure Silver Charm was getting the most from his time at Churchill, working his charge twice at five-eighths and once at three-quarters in the weeks leading up to the race. Based on pedigree, Silver Charm, a grandson of distance influences Poker and Buckpasser, had an advantage over Free House (whose sire, Smokester, was a sprinter), and a telling one at

In the Preakness, Silver Charm held off both Free House and Captain Bodgit.

Silver Charm had a Triple Crown in sight when Touch Gold snuck by on the outside.

that, as it would turn out.

On a Derby day as gray as the two rivals, Free House, who had drawn the outside post in the field of thirteen and was held at 10-1 by "show me" bettors, broke promptly under David Flores and inherited the lead, which he willingly surrendered to Pulpit in the first turn. Around the turn, Silver Charm, in midpack, survived being bumped by quickening away from a potential morass. Stevens had Silver Charm stalking close behind the leaders in perfect position.

With a quarter-mile to run, Free House passed Pulpit and held the lead turning into the stretch ever so briefly. Silver Charm pounced on him from the outside, gained the advantage, and, according to Stevens, "began goofing off." Perhaps Silver Charm, who Baffert said always needed someone to run

with, knew he had his old rival beaten, but what he didn't immediately see was Captain Bodgit flying down the middle of the track — not until the last, desperate fifty yards.

From there, it was sheer determination that carried Silver Charm to a head triumph, with Free House finishing 3½ lengths back in third.

Both colts came out of the race none the worse for the wear, and it was on to Baltimore and the Preakness. Here, Free House figured to have his best chance, in the shortest of the three Triple Crown races. He certainly arched some eyebrows four days before the contest when he worked an otherworldly half-mile in :45⅗. Gonzalez walked around in a state of shock, but, more important, the horse shrugged off his quick practice and ate up his feed that evening.

Baffert, meanwhile, with an eye on the three-race series, wanted to conserve as much of Silver Charm's energy as possible. "I didn't give him a sharp-enough work," he said, "so I was worried about that race."

Desormeaux, who had cut his teeth on the Maryland circuit with great success and knew Pimlico inside and out, was back aboard Free House for the Preakness with instructions not to make the lead too soon. Cryp Too took care of that by bouncing out front, and Free House set up camp just outside the lead. Silver Charm, amazingly sent off as the third choice, was again guided by Stevens into a perfect tracking perch behind the leaders.

After a half-mile, Desormeaux and Free House gained the lead and tried to steal away from Silver Charm, but the Derby winner quickened with him, and Desormeaux decided to slow things down ever so slightly. With an eighth of a mile to run, however, Desormeaux asked, and Free House delivered again, opening a length on Silver Charm.

And there they came, barreling down the stretch together, Free House holding his rival at bay, with only inches separating them. And then, Captain Bodgit joined the fray from the outside, making it a trio diving for the wire.

"I still think we should have won the Preakness," Toffan said eleven years later, "but we didn't, and that's the way it goes."

Said Stevens, "I had no idea if we were going to get to Free House. Fifty yards to go, and I had no idea who of the three was going to win. Captain Bodgit coming on the outside definitely helped Silver Charm. Silver Charm dug in for that battle and forgot about the battle he was having with Free House. He found that little extra he needed and just extended his neck."

Silver Charm defeated Free House by a head, with Captain Bodgit a head back of Free House in third. Silver Charm was still alive for a possible Triple Crown, but Free House had lost nothing in defeat.

"I'm as proud of him as I can be," McCaffery said, and the colt was on his way to New York and another date with his old pal.

Both horses continued to train well coming up to the Belmont Stakes. In front of 70,000 fans hoping to see the twelfth Triple Crown winner in history, Silver Charm and Free House put on a show. This time they ran in tandem most of the race. Into the first turn, Touch Gold had the lead and Free House was carried wide, just outside Silver Charm. Up the backstretch Wild Rush made the front, but these were merely preliminaries. The race was shaping up all along, it seemed, between Free House and Silver Charm.

On the final turn Wild Rush receded and Stevens remembers calling to Jerry Bailey, on Wild Rush, "Let the games begin." Stevens fired his big bullet. "I was hoping to blow right past Free House and not give him a chance to go heads up with me. I was surprised how easily Silver Charm went by Free House that day. And when he did go by, he eased up."

Free House stayed just close enough to Silver Charm that the latter did not see Touch Gold rallying on the outside. Having all the momentum as well as stealth in his favor, Touch Gold was on top of Silver Charm and the wire so quickly that the gray did not have time enough to react. By the time he dug back in, it was over, with Touch Gold winning by three-quarters of a length. Free House was another length back in third.

Stevens thought when he put away Free House, the race was his. "Had I not taken the rivalry so seriously and respected the entire field like I respected Free House, the outcome might have been different," he said. "But that's how much respect I had for Free House."

Irony abounds. Although Free House could not finish in front of Silver Charm in any of the Triple

Crown tests, his presence provided the cloak under which Touch Gold slipped into contention in the Belmont, ultimately denying Silver Charm the greater glory of the Triple Crown.

Nevertheless, it was a Triple Crown series for the ages. The two warriors had proven time and again their heart and determination. And though, as Baffert noted, there were similarities to the great wars waged by Ali and Frazier that took something out of the combatants, enough glory remained for both.

Just six weeks after the Belmont, Free House cruised to victory in the Swaps Stakes. After a ten-

month layoff that spanned the end of 1997 and half of 1998, he returned to take the Bel Air Handicap and the Pacific Classic in the summer of 1998.

Silver Charm, meanwhile, won two legs of the Strub series at Santa Anita to begin 1998, and then proved victorious in that year's Dubai World Cup, the world's richest race. After that journey, he seemed to have given up a step, losing his next two races and managing a dead heat for first with Wild Rush in the Kentucky Cup Classic Handicap, a race he figured to dominate.

So, it was October 1998 when Silver Charm returned home to California to meet Free House in

Silver Charm and Free House met for the seventh and penultimate time in the Goodwood Breeders' Cup Handicap.

the Goodwood Breeders' Cup Handicap, their seventh head-to-head tussle. Silver Charm stormed past Free House in the stretch of the Goodwood, easily defeating his foe by 2½ lengths.

After each enjoyed grade II victories early in 1999, they hooked up one last time, in the Santa Anita Handicap. Free House got the jump on Silver Charm that day, made the lead, and controlled the pace en route to victory, with Silver Charm a little more than a length away in third.

After a second in the Pimlico Special to 1998 Kentucky Derby victor Real Quiet in his next race, Free House was retired. He ended up with nine wins from twenty-two starts and earnings of $3,178,971.

Silver Charm boldly tried the Dubai World Cup again just weeks after the Santa Anita Handicap but came up empty there as well as in his final effort, the June 1999 Stephen Foster Handicap. His ledger showed twelve wins from twenty-four starts and purse winnings of $6,944,369.

After eight head-to-head tussles, the ledger ended with Silver Charm winning four, Free House three, and the pair finishing two-three in the Belmont.

There is little doubt what Silver Charm meant to the Lewises. In the home they shared in Newport Beach, California, before Bob's death in 2006, a Richard Stone Reeves oil painting of Silver Charm on the track at Churchill Downs looked down from a special place above the fireplace mantel, upon which his Eclipse Award sat.

When jockey Gary Stevens spoke for this chapter, he was in his home office, staring at a painting made from Dickstein's Preakness photograph.

Baffert recalled the days toward the end of Silver Charm's career when people started to say, "Maybe he was never that good." Baffert fixed a stare on his interviewer. "How can you say that about that horse?" he intoned. My attitude is, 'Don't you talk about that horse like that.' Not that horse."

After Free House died in a paddock accident in 2004, McCaffery said, "Of all the horses I've owned, he stands out because he had so much radiance to him. Everything he did, he did for fun. He loved to run, and he always tried hard. You don't get many horses like that, and with such charisma. It's like losing a son."

The 1997 Triple Crown season remains special for Baffert as well, though he enjoyed Kentucky Derby and Preakness victories with regularity after Silver Charm paved the way. "I think they were both freaks of nature," he said of Silver Charm and Free House. "The pedigrees didn't say they were supposed to be that good. They were two gray horses that outran their pedigrees. And every time they ran, they gave everything they had. Those kind of horses are hard to come by."

Classic
Confrontations

BY SEAN CLANCY

Steve Asmussen's eyes widened — and they're already wide. The record-breaking, globe-trotting trainer pushed off the wooden rail he had been leaning on outside the stakes barn at Pimlico Racecourse and began animating what he had witnessed on that third Saturday in May. The traditional after-Preakness party rollicked at the end of the stakes barn, but it had nothing on Asmussen. His hands waved, his voice quivered, his friends and family stopped to listen. A horse trainer by trade and a racing fan at heart, Asmussen knew he had seen brilliance.

"Nobody will be disappointed in that running of the Preakness. He was 100 percent all out and showed his greatness by getting by the Derby winner, a great horse, in an excellent time," Asmussen said. "If these horses stay around, that will be one of those charts to look back at and say, 'Look who was in that race.'"

The 2007 Preakness marked the second time in two weeks that Curlin, Street Sense, and Hard Spun had finished one, two, three. Two weeks, two classics, same three finishers, different order — charts that will be looked back upon with awe.

The Breeders' Cup Classic reunited the Derby and Preakness rivals, with Curlin triumphing in the muddy going.

Hard Spun put up audacious fractions, but Street Sense engulfed him with his centripetal rally on the turn. Then in a matter of a furlong, Curlin became a man, nailing the Kentucky Derby winner on the line. Curlin by a head over Street Sense with the gallant Hard Spun hanging tough to finish third, four lengths behind his rivals. In his fifth career start, Curlin had equaled the Preakness Stakes record set by Louis Quatorze and Tank's Prospect of 1:53⅖.

In retrospect, the Preakness would become — collectively — the threesome's finest hour.

Curlin, Street Sense, and Hard Spun went their separate ways after the Preakness, each collecting grade I scores that would further attest to their talent. They met once more — appropriately in the Breeders' Cup Classic at Monmouth Park in November. By then, Curlin had distanced himself from the rest, showing his prowess in the Classic. He dominated Hard Spun, who held on for second with Street Sense fading to finish fourth in the year's finale. In the dying light at Monmouth Park, Street Sense failed to round out the trifecta for the first time in his career, an unjust finish as the year belonged to him and his brothers in arms, Curlin and Hard Spun.

Still, Curlin earned the Eclipse Award as top three-year-old and Horse of the Year. Hard Spun and Street Sense collectively earned more than $7 million for their roles as the star's supporting actors.

The trio served up a rare and potent cocktail in today's climate, doing battle from May to October. They separated on occasion — Street Sense sweeping the Travers and Jim Dandy, Curlin taking the Jockey Club Gold Cup, and Hard Spun sprinting to win the King's Bishop — but then converged on racing's biggest days. They threw their punches. They ducked no one, let alone each other.

Street Sense triumphed over Hard Spun, No. 8, and Curlin in the Derby.

Curlin wore down Street Sense in a heart-thumping edition of the Preakness Stakes.

As the two-year-old crop turned three, Street Sense led the battalion. The strapping first-crop son of Street Cry had punished his rivals at Churchill Downs in the 2006 Breeders' Cup Juvenile, clinching his Eclipse Award. Trainer Carl Nafzger had primed Street Sense for his two-year-old goal, and the colt hadn't disappointed, streaking through on the rail to win by ten lengths under Calvin Borel.

Nafzger knew he had something special long before the 2006 Breeders' Cup. Street Sense had earned the trainer's regard back in the spring,

months away from his first race. So much so that the sixty-four-year-old veteran trainer couldn't contain himself as he gave Borel his first leg up on Street Sense to breeze an easy half-mile that spring.

"This is our big horse," Nafzger had boldly told Borel as the jockey adjusted his irons.

"Now, Carl doesn't say things like that," Borel remembered.

In about thirty-four seconds, Borel knew why he had said it.

Street Sense loped into his long stride, airing

three furlongs in :34 and galloping out in :47 and change. Borel could barely pull him up.

"Oh, what I got here. He was jumping from here to that table," Borel said, pointing to a jocks' room table about thirty feet away. "When I stood up and galloped out, it was unbelievable, scary. I slowed him down and said, 'oh Lord, no more.' I'll never forget that feeling, oooh, Lord."

Nafzger unveiled Jim Tafel's homebred in a maiden special weight at Churchill Downs in July. He beat nine rivals but proved no match for Unbridled Express, finishing four lengths adrift in second. Given more than five weeks until his next start, Street Sense handled maidens at Arlington Park in August then weakened late in the Arlington Futurity, finishing third. In his next start he reached the lead and then fumbled it, winding up third in the Lane's End Breeders' Futurity at Keeneland. His Breeders' Cup tour de force anointed him as the two-year-old champ, and he finished the year as the next potential-laden youngster that would try to defy the Breeders' Cup Juvenile jinx. No horse had won the Juvenile and the Derby, and few had amounted to anything more than one-hit wonders that posted a big two-year-old season but never replicated the feat.

Street Sense, at least, appeared different. He had old-school Nafzger in his kitchen, and he had breeding, scope, size, and stability on his side. He wasn't a jet-fueled baby that had simply developed quicker; he possessed all the jewels. Part philosopher, part horse trainer, Nafzger could even pinpoint his assets.

"He's got the four traits of a winner: ability, soundness, mental, immune system," Nafzger said during the off-season. "What welds them all together is class."

While Street Sense erected his two-for-five championship season at two, trainer Larry Jones mapped out a different course for Hard Spun. A Pennsylvania-bred son of Danzig, Hard Spun followed former three-year-old stars Afleet Alex and Barbaro, breaking his maiden at Delaware Park. Owned by Rick Porter's Fox Hill Farms and ridden by Mario Pino, Hard Spun had humbled seven foes, cruising to an 8¾-length victory.

Jones, taking off his cowboy hat and galloping the horse himself, kept to his conservative route, sending Hard Spun to win the Port Penn at Delaware in his next start. Hard Spun finished the year with another impressive victory, taking the Pennsylvania Nursery by 7¾ lengths. A tall, but compact, bay colt, Hard Spun had breeding on his side, too. Bred by Michael Moran and Brushwood Stable, Hard Spun carried the waning genes of the great pensioned stallion Danzig and carried the stamina of Turkoman on his dam's side.

As the Derby Trail filled up with Street Sense, Hard Spun, and every other two-year-old phenom, Curlin hadn't made his first start as winter set in and routes were mapped for the first Saturday in May. Bred in Kentucky by Fares Farm, Curlin had attracted trainer Ken McPeek's astute eye at the Keeneland September yearling sale in 2005. McPeek ignored an osteochondrosis (OCD) lesion that had been removed from Curlin's left front ankle and bought the stout son of Smart Strike for $57,000 on behalf of Shirley Cunningham Jr.'s and William Gallion's Midnight Cry Stable.

McPeek subsequently embarked on a sabbatical from training, and Midnight Cry Stable turned Curlin over to McPeek's assistant, Helen Pitts, who was thrust into the starter's role when McPeek packed up. From a long line of Maryland horsemen, Pitts took her time with Curlin, revving him up and then simmering him down while the talented colt tried to grow into his massive frame. Curlin bucked his shins twice and finally made his debut at Gulfstream

Park in February. He won by 12¾ lengths and looked more like a towel on tumble dry than a professional racehorse. He did it on ability alone.

Then Pitts' phone started ringing. Maidens didn't win like that. Bloodstock agent John Moynihan smelled a horse deal and started working on a partnership, ultimately delivering the horse to Asmussen under the ownership umbrella of Jess Jackson's Stonestreet Stable, Satish Sanan's Padua Stable, George Bolton, and Midnight Cry Stable.

That's when the fun started.

As Curlin started breezing for Asmussen, the Texas-born trainer never considered an allowance race, sending Curlin to Oaklawn Park, where he swept the Rebel and the Arkansas Derby. Under Robby Albarado, Curlin toyed with more experienced rivals, winning the Rebel by 5½ lengths and the Arkansas Derby by a whopping 10½ lengths. Next stop, Louisville.

"He does things normal horses don't do. We brought him in the barn and asked him questions through training, if he was good enough for the Rebel. He answered them emphatically," Asmussen said. "You walked over there thinking you had the best horse and that's been the case every time. What would you be waiting on if you didn't run him? The next one? That's how you feel. Who do you want to run in there? I want to run him."

No doubt, Nafzger wanted to run Street Sense.

With a battle-tested five starts notched in his belt as a two-year-old, Street Sense didn't need seasoning or experience. Nafzger played it cool, mapping out two starts before the Derby.

He shipped Street Sense to Tampa Bay Downs for the Tampa Bay Derby. It was the colt's first fight. In his five starts at two, Street Sense either streaked past his competition or on two occasions blinked when he should have buckled down. In the Tampa Bay Derby, he hooked Any Given Saturday, and they

slugged it out down the stretch. Street Sense managed to get his nose down to win his three-year-old debut. Nafzger couldn't have planned it better.

"Eyeball to eyeball; that's what we saw in the Tampa Bay Derby. I didn't know if I had a dog-eat-dog until then," Nafzger said. "He'd either bowl to the lead or in the Breeders' Cup, he shot to the lead. Nobody had latched into him and said, 'Let's see what you got.' A heart check. We saw that in the Tampa Bay Derby."

Nafzger confidently shipped north to Kentucky and took aim at the Blue Grass Stakes. Over Keeneland's Polytrack surface, Street Sense couldn't nail down the last major Derby prep, failing by a nose to Dominican in a seven-horse jamboree at the wire. Nafzger tossed the result — run at a dawdling time — filed the race as a decent breeze, and set sail for Churchill Downs.

While Curlin roared through Arkansas and Street Sense took his deliberate steps to the Derby, Hard Spun was doing little wrong. Jones had put Hard Spun on a once-a-month diet of progressively more difficult challenges. Hard Spun took the Le Comte at Fair Grounds in January and then settled in at Oaklawn Park for a Midwest campaign. Hard Spun entered the Southwest undefeated but squandered the race with a lackluster fourth to the unheralded Teuflesberg, Officer Rocket, and Forty Grams. Jones decided to get out of town, chalking up the loss to the track.

Hard Spun made his Polytrack debut in the Lane's End at Turfway Park, and he quickly dismissed the Southwest debacle, rolling to an easy win and upping his gaudy record to five for six.

Finally, May 5 arrived. Street Sense, Curlin, and Hard Spun would all meet for the first time — in the Derby.

Street Sense attracted the most attention, going off as the 4.90-1 favorite. Bettors forgave Curlin's

The filly Rags to Riches, outside, refused to yield to Curlin in the Belmont Stakes.

Hard Spun led throughout in the Kentucky Cup Classic, with Street Sense not being asked for his best effort.

inexperience, pounding him to second choice at 5-1, and Hard Spun collected his share of followers, going off at 10-1.

Jockey Pino ended all pace discussion, sending Hard Spun to the front of the twenty-horse field. Albarado guided Curlin from post two and found a spot in thirteenth while Borel perched motionless in his acey-deucey stirrups, allowing Street Sense free rein to lag in nineteenth, nearly twenty lengths from Hard Spun.

Hard Spun had the field on the run as he turned for home with a commanding lead. Street Sense led a parade of one, zipping through on the rail to run down Hard Spun inside the furlong pole. Borel stood high in his irons and saluted the racing gods as Street Sense streaked home by 2¼ lengths over Hard Spun, with Curlin galloping to the line in third. Street Sense was brilliant. Hard Spun, gallant. Curlin, a day late and a dollar short.

That was the last day Curlin was late.

Not that Nafzger could see it. Coming off the Derby, he was as confident as a dog in a cat fight.

"He's finally fit; I've finally got his mind. If nothing goes wrong, you'll see the best Street Sense. It's a scary feeling," Nafzger said, hours before the Preakness. "If everything goes right and he doesn't

CURLIN – STREET SENSE – HARD SPUN

fire, they'll get me on TV, just standing there, thinking, 'What could I have missed with this horse?' "

Turns out, Nafzger didn't miss a thing. His horse ran his race just as he had in his previous eight starts. It was just that Curlin ran a little bit better. Exactly a head better, snuffing out the chances of a Triple Crown winner but doing nothing to diminish the three-year-old crop of 2007.

Breaking from post four in the Preakness, Curlin buckled when the gates opened, spotting ground to his eight rivals and giving Albarado the same sickening feeling he had going into the first turn of the Derby when the race's tempo moved quicker than Curlin's brain could process.

Albarado niggled at the chestnut colt, who stubbornly stayed on his left lead for the first furlong, just to keep pace with the late-running Street Sense. Under the wire the first time, Curlin found his spot in sixth, a notch in front of Street Sense.

Pino rated Hard Spun behind Xchanger and Flying First Class and then put on his blinker to roar into the lead leaving the backside. On the turn Curlin tracked in third, to the outside of C P West and Hard Spun. Albarado braced against Curlin, who was cornering more like a hook and ladder than a Preakness winner. Calvin Borel guided Street Sense between the retreating Xchanger and King of the Roxy into fourth, poised for that move he knew so well.

Street Sense rolled past Curlin and then swept past Hard Spun just as he had done in the Derby.

In the stands, Nafzger nudged Tafel, believing he was seeing exactly what he expected from Street Sense. Albarado stayed the course on Curlin, riding and balancing at the same time, and just hoping to get out of the turn within eyesight of Street Sense.

In the Derby, Street Sense had accelerated past Curlin in a flash. That day, Albarado knew it was over. In the Preakness, Street Sense had never

gotten away. Albarado had cued Curlin to switch to his right lead, and when he did, Street Sense was still in range.

Inside the sixteenth pole, Borel wasn't nudging anyone as he looked over his right shoulder, seeing exactly what he feared — the resolute Curlin. At the wire, Albarado rose in his stirrups, raising his whip momentarily before cutting it through the air in triumph. The Triple Crown of 2007 was over.

With the disappointment waging heartburn in Nafzger's chest, the trainer immediately began planning a summer campaign rather than a van ride to Belmont Park to settle the Triple Crown standoff with Curlin. Asmussen and Jones took a few days to observe their pupils and then went full speed ahead to Belmont.

Curlin hooked Kentucky Oaks winner Rags to Riches in the Belmont Stakes, just missing to the filly, who further emboldened the three-year-old crop as one of the best in history. Ridden for the first time by Garrett Gomez, Hard Spun sat in no-man's land and eventually succumbed to the pace scenario.

Nafzger couldn't have planned his summer better, feeding on Saratoga's menu of the Jim Dandy and the Travers while Curlin and Hard Spun met yet again in the Haskell at Monmouth where neither produced his best. Hard Spun salvaged second, a head in front of Curlin but well off the fresh Any Given Saturday.

After the Haskell, Jones decided to seek other opportunities, landing on the seven-furlong King's Bishop at Saratoga.

"Rick wanted to get his grade I win in and he asked me where the best shot was, I said 'wherever Street Sense and Curlin are not,' " Jones said. "The King's Bishop was coming up; get me away from them just one time. I was tired of feeling like Sham."

Curlin's Classic victory secured his Horse of the Year honors.

Hard Spun showed his class by turning back from nine furlongs to seven furlongs, taking the King's Bishop. Then it was back to big game.

The last weekend of September, Hard Spun and Street Sense squared off in the Kentucky Cup at Turfway Park while Curlin went after older horses in the Jockey Club Gold Cup.

Hard Spun handled Street Sense, setting the pace and holding off his old friend in what amounted to a perfect prep for both horses leading to the Breeders'

Cup Classic a month later.

A day after the Kentucky Cup, Curlin met Whitney and Woodward stakes winner Lawyer Ron in the 1¼-mile classic at Belmont Park. Curlin wore down Lawyer Ron to win by a neck. Amazingly, it was his first victory since the Preakness.

The three rivals were all set for their final showdown in the Breeders' Cup Classic at Monmouth Park. Rain added an asterisk to the day's races, but Curlin put the period on the final sentence.

Turning for home in the 1¼-mile stakes, the three horses found themselves in their customary spots. Hard Spun, on the lead awaiting the challenges that he had grown to know. Curlin, bridging the gap between Hard Spun and Street Sense. And Street Sense, honing in on his two rivals.

Then suddenly it was over. Hard Spun wavered. Street Sense hung. And Curlin powered home alone, ending all debate over who was best.

"You never saw one of them weak," Asmussen said. "Every time you watched them train, you're like, 'you better be ready because they're ready.' I loved that. I loved the dominance they showed outside of their own group. I loved the fact that even when they got beat, you'd know they were showing up the next time. There was no upper hand. Curlin came out on top at the end of the year, but I think it was simply ability. Education-wise, he caught up to them."

By April 2008, only Curlin still faced the test of time. Darley whisked Street Sense and Hard Spun to the stallion barn while Curlin shipped to Dubai to take on the world. Curlin showed that his growth curve was still on the rise, winning the Jaguar Trophy and then decimating the Dubai World Cup field. Asmussen had said goodbye to Curlin's old rivals and welcomed his new ones.

"When you stand there and think of Curlin's Horse of the Year season, what makes it is Street Sense and Hard Spun. And the fact that in today's day and age they were there so many times, you don't see that," Asmussen said.

"You're talking about rivalries. There are no rivalries anymore; everybody avoids everybody now. Nobody batted an eye; everybody showed up. I never saw any of them have a bad day. I have enduring respect for the group. You want to look back at these charts and say, 'Man, look who ran against who.' It was one of those years."

Leaders Lists

Round Table is tops.

MOST WINS (OVER 20)

HORSE	WINS
Round Table	43
Armed	41
Kelso	39
Stymie	35
Nashua	22
Gallorette	21

UNBEATEN

HORSE	WINS
Colin	15
Personal Ensign	13

MOST STARTS (OVER 50)

HORSE	STARTS
Stymie	131
Seabiscuit	89
Armed	81
Gallorette	72
Round Table	66
Kelso	63
Equipoise	51

KENTUCKY DERBY WINNERS

HORSE	YEAR
Twenty Grand	1931
War Admiral	1937
Assault	1946
Majestic Prince	1969
Affirmed	1978
Alysheba	1987
Sunday Silence	1989
Silver Charm	1997
Street Sense	2006

PREAKNESS STAKES WINNERS

HORSE	YEAR
War Admiral	1937
Assault	1946
Nashua	1955
Bold Ruler	1957
Damascus	1967
Majestic Prince	1969
Affirmed	1978
Alysheba	1987
Sunday Silence	1989
Silver Charm	1997
Curlin	2007

BELMONT STAKES WINNERS

HORSE	YEAR
Henry of Navarre	1894
Colin	1908
Twenty Grand	1931
War Admiral	1937
Assault	1946
Nashua	1955
Gallant Man	1957
Jaipur	1962
Damascus	1967
Arts and Letters	1969
Affirmed	1978
Bet Twice	1987
Easy Goer	1989

Henry of Navarre
is the earliest Belmont winner.

Curlin, left, and Street Sense rank
1st and 4th on the earnings list.

LEADING EARNERS
(OVER $1,000,000)

HORSE	TOTAL EARNINGS
Curlin	$9,396,800*
Silver Charm	$6,944,369
Alysheba	$6,679,242
Street Sense	$6,516,158
Sunday Silence	$4,968,554
Easy Goer	$4,873,770
Free House	$3,178,971
Hard Spun	$2,673,470
Affirmed	$2,393,818
Kelso	$1,977,896
Personal Ensign	$1,679,880
Winning Colors	$1,526,837
Nashua	$1,288,565
Damascus	$1,176,781
Dr. Fager	$1,002,642

* As of June 14, 2008

CHAMPIONS

Affirmed
(ch.c. 1975 Exclusive Native—Won't Tell You, by Crafty Admiral)
- **1977 2yo male**
- **1978 3yo male, Horse of the Year**
- **1979 handicap male, Horse of the Year**

Affirmed was a three-time champion.

Alysheba
(b.c. 1984 Alydar—Bel Sheba, by Lt. Stevens)
- **1987 3yo male**
- **1988 handicap male, Horse of the Year**

Armed
(br.g. 1941 Bull Lea—Armful, by Chance Shot)
- **1946 handicap male**
- **1947 handicap male, Horse of the Year**

Arts and Letters
(ch.c. 1966 Ribot—All Beautiful, by Battlefield)
- **1969 3yo male, handicap male, Horse of the Year**

Assault
(ch.c. 1943 Bold Venture—Igual, by Equipoise)
- **1946 3yo male, Horse of the Year**

Bed o' Roses
(b.f. 1947 Rosemont—Good Thing, by Discovery)
- **1949 2yo filly**
- **1951 handicap female**

Bold Ruler
(dk b/br. c. 1954 Nasrullah—Miss Disco, by Discovery)
- **1957 3yo male, Horse of the Year**
- **1958 sprinter**

Clifford
(br. c. 1890 Bramble—Duchess, by
- **1893 3yo male**
- **1894 handicap male**

Colin
(b. c. 1905 Commando—Pastorella, by Springfield)
- **1907 2yo male, Horse of the Year**
- **1908 3yo male, Horse of the Year**

Curlin
(ch.c. 2004 Smart Strike—Sherrif's Deputy, by Deputy Minister)
- **2007 3yo male, Horse of the Year**

Damascus
(b.c. 1964 Sword Dancer—Kerala, by My Babu)
- **1967 3yo male, handicap male, Horse of the Year**

Domino
(dk. b/br.c. 1891 Commando—Mannie Gray, by Enquirer)
- **1893 2yo male, Horse of the Year**
- **1894 3yo male**

Dr. Fager
(b.c. 1964 Rough'n Tumble—Aspidistra, by Better Self)
- **1967 sprinter**
- **1968 handicap male, turf male, sprinter, Horse of the Year**

Easy Goer
(ch.c. 1986 Alydar—Relaxing, by Buckpasser)
- **1988 2yo male**

Equipoise
(ch.c. 1928 Pennant—Swinging, by Broomstick)
- **1930 2yo male**
- **1932 handicap male, Horse of the Year**
- **1933 handicap male, Horse of the Year**
- **1934 handicap male**

Gallorette
(ch.c. 1942 Challenger II—Gallette, by Sir Gallahad III)
- **1946 handicap female**

CHAMPIONS

Kelso was a 5-time Champion.

Henry of Navarre
(ch.c. 1891 Knight of Ellerslie—Moss Rose, by The Ill-Used)
- **1894** 3yo male, Horse of the Year
- **1895** handicap male, Horse of the Year
- **1896** handicap male

Jaipur
(dk b/br.c. 1959 Nasrullah—Rare Perfume, by Eight Thirty)
- **1962** 3yo male

Kelso
(dk b/br. g. 1957 Your Host—Maid of Flight, by Count Fleet)
- **1960** 3yo male, Horse of the Year
- **1961** handicap male, Horse of the Year
- **1962** handicap male, Horse of the Year
- **1963** handicap male, Horse of the Year
- **1964** handicap male, Horse of the Year

Next Move
(br.f. 1947 Bull Lea—Now What, by Chance Shot)
- **1950** 3yo filly
- **1952** handicap female

Personal Ensign
(b.f. 1984 Private Account—Grecian Banner, by Hoist the Flag)
- **1988** handicap female, Broodmare of the Year

Ridan
(b.c. 1959 Nantallah—Rough Shod II, by Gold Bridge)
- **1961** 2yo male

Round Table
(b.c. 1954 Princequillo—Knight's Daughter, by Sir Cosmo)
- **1957** turf male
- **1958** handicap male, turf male, Horse of the Year
- **1959** handicap male, turf male

Seabiscuit
(b.c. 1933 Hard Tack—Swing On, by Whisk Broom II)
- **1937** handicap male
- **1938** handicap male, Horse of the Year

Silver Charm
(gr/ro.c. 1994 Silver Buck—Bonnie's Poker, by Poker)
- **1997** 3yo male, highweighted older horse UAE

Street Sense
(dk b/br.c. 2004 Street Cry [Ire]—Bedazzle, by Dixieland Band)
- **2006** 2yo male

Stymie
(ch.c. 1941 Equestrian—Stop Watch, by On Watch)
- **1945** handicap male

Sunday Silence
(dk b/br.c. 1986 Halo—Wishing Well, by Understanding)
- **1989** 3yo male, Horse of the Year

Twenty Grand
(b.c. 1928 St. Germans—Bonus, by All Gold)
- **1931** 3yo male, Horse of the Year

War Admiral
(br.c. 1934 Man o' War—Brushup, by Sweep)
- **1937** 3yo male, Horse of the Year

Winning Colors
(ro.f. 1985 Caro [Ire]—All Rainbows, by Bold Hour)
- **1988** 3yo filly

Photo Credits

About the Authors

Rena Baer

Baer is a Lexington-based freelance writer and editor whose work has appeared in *Keeneland* magazine and other publications.

George Bernet

A former writer for and editor-in-chief of *Daily Racing Form*, Bernet is a member of Monmouth Park's publicity staff.

Edward L. Bowen

Bowen is the award-winning author of eighteen books on horse racing, including *Legacies of the Turf* (vols. I & II) and biographies of Man o' War and Bold Ruler. Bowen is also president of the Grayson-Jockey Club Research Foundation.

Sean Clancy

Clancy, a former champion steeplechase jockey, is an award-winning author whose latest work, *Barbaro: The Horse Who Captured America's Heart,* received a 2008 Benjamin Franklin Award.

Tracy Gantz

Gantz is managing editor of John Lyons' *Perfect Horse* magazine and a correspondent for *The Blood-Horse* magazine. She began her career at *The Blood-Horse* and also served as the West Coast breeding columnist for *Daily Racing Form.*

Scot T. Gillies

Gillies is research editor for digital media at Blood-Horse Publications and is a Thoroughbred breeder. He is a frequent contributor to *Keeneland* magazine.

Tom Hall

Hall is managing editor of Eclipse Press and has contributed work to a number of horse racing books.

Avalyn Hunter

Hunter is a mental health professional and Thoroughbred pedigree researcher. She is the author of *American Classic Pedigrees* and biographies of two of the modern breed's most influential stallions *Kingmaker* (Northern Dancer) and *Gold Rush* (Mr. Prospector).

Michele MacDonald

MacDonald is a Lexington-based writer who has earned multiple awards for her writing. Her work has been published in a number of periodicals in the United States, Great Britain, and Dubai.

Judy L. Marchman

Marchman is assistant editor of the *Texas Bar Journal*, the official publication of the State Bar of Texas, and a frequent contributor to many horse racing books. She is also the editor of *Kentucky Derby Glasses Price Guide*.

John McEvoy

A former Midwest editor and senior writer for *Daily Racing Form*, McEvoy is a well-known Turf writer and author of several books including the award-winning *Great Horse Racing Mysteries*, a biography of Round Table, and *Women in Racing*, which he co-authored with his daughter, Julia McEvoy. He also writes mysteries.

Eliza McGraw

McGraw is a freelance writer living in Washington, D.C. Her work has appeared in *The Blood-Horse, EQUUS,* and the *Washington Post*. She is also the author of *Everyday Horsemanship*.

Lenny Shulman

Shulman, an Emmy Award-winning writer and producer, is features editor for *The Blood-Horse*. His book, *Ride of Their Lives*, chronicles the lives of many of racing's most prominent jockeys

Gary West

West is a sportswriter and horse racing columnist for the Fort Worth (Texas) *Star-Telegram* and is author of *Razoo at the Races*, a humorous look at horse racing and handicappers.

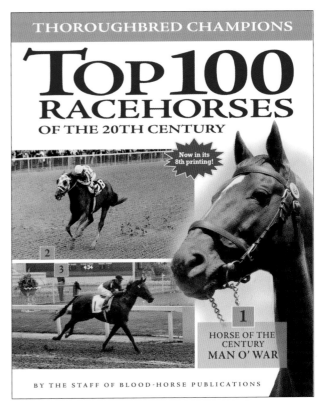